BEER HIKING
CANADIAN ROCKIES

THE TASTIEST WAY TO DISCOVER THE MOUNTAIN RANGES
OF ALBERTA AND BRITISH COLUMBIA

Beer Hiking Canadian Rockies
The Tastiest Way to Discover the Mountain Ranges
of Alberta and British Columbia
By: Kendall Hunter

ISBN: 9783907293898
Published by Helvetiq, Lausanne/Basel, Switzerland
Cover Design: Ajša Zdravković
Graphic Design and illustration: Daniel Malak, Jędrzej Malak (maps)
Printed in China
First edition: May 2023

info@helvetiq.ch

www.helvetiq.com
www.facebook.com/helvetiq
instagram: @helvetiq

helvetiq.com

BEER HIKING
CANADIAN ROCKIES

THE TASTIEST WAY TO DISCOVER THE MOUNTAIN RANGES OF ALBERTA AND BRITISH COLUMBIA

TABLE OF CONTENTS

1

INTRODUCTION

ABOUT THE AUTHOR

Kendall grew up in Banff National Park in Alberta, and the hiking trails and ski slopes of the area were her backyard playground. She learned to walk and ski simultaneously—frozen diapers and all—when her parents strapped skis to her feet when she was all of thirteen months old. Throughout her teenage years, she was a competitive ski racer, training in the French and Italian Alps and on the perennial snowfields of the American Pacific Northwest during the off-season, and competing in the Rockies every winter.

In Kendall's final semester as a political science major at the University of Calgary, she worked in Johannesburg as a news photographer for an independent Black newspaper. At the time, South Africa was preparing for its first democratic elections. She was asked by her editor to stay on through the elections, and thus covered one of the most important stories of the 20th century: the demise of apartheid rule in South Africa. Kendall's first book, *Black Taxi: Shooting South Africa*, is a photographic memoir about her experience. She wrote her second book,

Switzerland: The Essential Guide to Customs & Culture, for the Culture Smart series while raising a family in Zurich. She returned to her hometown in the Rockies in 2009 with her two daughters and began working on her next project, a memoir about traveling with her children to meet some of the world's top women photojournalists. After a few years in Toronto, where she ventured into the start-up world with plans to develop an online platform for traditional artisans, Kendall once again felt the pull of the Rockies. In 2022, she learned about the *Beer Hiking* series. Realizing that there were few better places for hiking and beer than her old stomping grounds, she headed west to explore the trails and develop a taste for the Rockies' finest craft beer. Kendall prefers dark porters like the All-Nighter Vanilla Cappuccino from Cold Garden Brewery in Calgary, but she has also come to appreciate a dry, crisp pilsner at the end of the trail. Now that she's decided to stay on in Banff for a while, she's thrilled that one of her favs, Banff Avenue Brewing Company's Ride or Dry, is on tap just down the road.

Kendall has a passion for writing about issues of social justice, especially in relation to women and girls. For several years now, she has been a features contributor for the Women's Media Center's online site (founded by Gloria Steinem, Jane Fonda, and Robin Morgan) in the US. When Kendall is not writing, she's probably doing her next favorite thing: focusing her camera on the paradoxes and natural beauty of the world around her.

ABOUT BEER HIKING IN THE CANADIAN ROCKIES

Beer may have been introduced to Canada by European settlers, but it's now as much a part of Canadian identity as bacon and maple syrup. It became entrenched in our popular culture by the toque-wearing TV duo Doug and Bob McKenzie, who first appeared on air in the early 80s, satirizing Canadians while sitting next to a towering stack of Molson Canadian lager. Canada is also known for its great outdoors, and the diversity of the Canadian natural world is nowhere more on display than in the Canadian Rockies. Upwards of nine million people visit the Rockies annually to explore the peaks, grasslands, forested valleys, beautiful blue rivers, turquoise lakes, and wetlands of Alberta and British Columbia (BC). Here they find a wide variety of trails suited to a broad range of abilities, with rewards of breathtaking views from summits and bluffs and wildlife sightings at every turn.

The Canadian Rockies consist of the 1,500-kilometer segment of the Rocky Mountains that straddles the border between Alberta and British Columbia in Western Canada. They are also home to Canada's oldest and best-known national park, Banff National Park—as well as to Yoho, Kootenay, and Jasper National Parks, which have all been declared UNESCO World Heritage Sites. Geologically speaking, the Canadian Rocky Mountain system doesn't include the ranges west of the Rocky Mountain Trench (the Columbia Mountains), but due to their proximity, many still consider them part of the "Rockies." Since there are some fabulous craft breweries nesting on the slopes of the Columbia Mountains and in the valleys around it, it would have been remiss of me not to bring this region into the fold. I've also included the city of Calgary and its neighboring foothills, often referred to as the "gateway to the Rockies." This is ranching country, after all, and the home of the world-renowned Calgary Stampede—and what cowboy doesn't enjoy a cold beer after a long day on the trail?

Molson may still be loved by Canadians, but since Doug and Bob left the airwaves, the beer-brewing landscape has undergone a sea change. Canada's first microbreweries opened in 1984, and their kind increasingly dot the maps of both Alberta and BC. Generally founded by outdoor enthusiasts who love their beer, the craft breweries in the mountains benefit from nature's most precious gift—pure water. In the interior of the Rockies, brew masters are truly serving up communion with nature as they deftly divert glacial melt into their tanks and onto your palate in every kind of beer—from pale ale to dark chocolate stout. It doesn't get any better than this!

In this book, the names of Europeans will often come up in association with roads and mountains in the Rockies and Europeans will occasionally be credited with the "discovery" of a certain lake or the "settlement" of a particular region during their work for entities such as the North West Company, the Hudson's Bay Company, and the Canadian Pacific Railway. Let us pay tribute to the heritage and legacy of Canada's aboriginal people, however, by acknowledging that these "discoveries" and "settlements" in fact took place on the treaty lands and territories of numerous and diverse First Nations—people who had known the area intimately for millennia and treated it with far more respect and dignity than the European colonizers and industrialists who began arriving in the early 17th century.

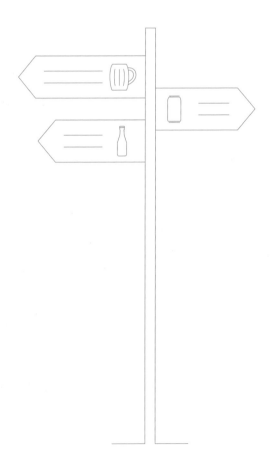

CHOOSE THE BEER OR THE HIKE

HIKE LOCATION ──────→

REGION ──────────

MAP ──────────→

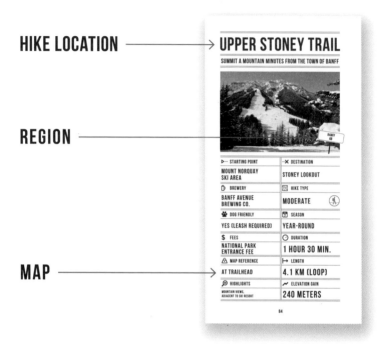

UPPER STONEY TRAIL

SUMMIT A MOUNTAIN MINUTES FROM THE TOWN OF BANFF

▷ STARTING POINT	✕ DESTINATION
MOUNT NORQUAY SKI AREA	STONEY LOOKOUT
🍺 BREWERY	🥾 HIKE TYPE
BANFF AVENUE BREWING CO.	MODERATE
🐾 DOG FRIENDLY	📅 SEASON
YES (LEASH REQUIRED)	YEAR-ROUND
$ FEES	⏲ DURATION
NATIONAL PARK ENTRANCE FEE	1 HOUR 30 MIN.
⚠ MAP REFERENCE	↦ LENGTH
AT TRAILHEAD	4.1 KM (LOOP)
🔍 HIGHLIGHTS	〰 ELEVATION GAIN
MOUNTAIN VIEWS, ADJACENT TO SKI RESORT	240 METERS

84

NAME OF THE BEER ←──────

INFORMATION ABOUT THE BEER ←──────

INFORMATION ABOUT THE HIKE ←──────

ON THE HIKES AND HIKE RATINGS

The hikes in this book have been rated as easy, moderate, or strenuous, and you'll be told whether a given hike is a loop or a round-trip (out and back the same way). Occasionally, I will also suggest alternative routes. I've made a point of choosing a wide variety of trails suited for all abilities and interests. Some easy trails may appear very short, but these often feature interpretive signs and unique ecosystems where you'll benefit from taking your time and absorbing impressions of the wildlife and fauna around you.

Generally, if a hike is relatively flat, with little elevation gain, it's rated as easy. This book features an abundance of moderate hikes, offering a solid variety of terrain with rewarding views and enough time left to fit in a substantial brewery visit. I've thrown in a few strenuous hikes as well; these make you work for that beer at the end and will really get your heart pumping. They may be shorter than some moderate hikes in terms of distance but often feature significant elevation gains—because sometimes, you've just gotta get high in the Rockies!

 EASY

 MODERATE

 STRENUOUS

ON THE BREWERIES AND BEER RATINGS

With just a few exceptions, the selected breweries are located half an hour or less from the trailheads. The days and hours of operation vary; all breweries are open daily or nearly so. Almost all breweries allow dogs, if not in the restaurant or taproom, then on the patio. All promote a family-friendly atmosphere and offer non-alcoholic options, and children are always welcome. I recommend checking the hours of operation when planning your hike, since some breweries don't open until late in the day and some have differing winter and summer hours. Check the brewery's website—or even better, in many cases, its social media pages—for the most up-to-date information.

The beer featured with each hike might be that brewery's flagship brew, its most popular offering, a recommendation to the author by bar staff or a patron on the next bar stool, something fun or funky that caught her eye, or a brew that simply fit the location or the weather on the day of her visit. Beer ratings are subjective. The color, aroma, taste, bitterness, and sweetness assigned to the highlighted beers are based on conversations with the brewers and brewery owners, as well as the author's tasting notes. As with the rated difficulty of the hikes, however, your individual experience with the beers may be a little or a lot different. The fact is that there's a wealth of really good beer to be enjoyed all over the Rockies, from the more traditional beers—the lagers, IPAs, wheat beers, porters, and stouts—to the fruit sours and other specialty brews, experimental batches, and one-offs. Most breweries feature a tap list of regularly available beers, which the author has chosen the featured brew from. Others have constantly rotating offerings. But what you can always count on is variety and that you'll find one or more beers that will delight your olfactory senses and satisfy your taste buds. Talk with the brewery staff and ask for a taster or two, or consider ordering a flight or sample tray, which is a good way to try a few different brews before selecting a full pour.

Access to most of the trails and breweries in this book requires a vehicle. Please enjoy your brews responsibly. Allow at least 45 minutes per beer consumed for your system to process the alcohol before driving. Better yet is to have a designated driver. Another option is to grab a growler, crowler, or fourpack to go and enjoy your beer safely, responsibly, and comfortably back at home, at your campsite, or in your cabin, hotel room, or RV.

PREPARING FOR YOUR HIKE

THE ESSENTIALS

1. Be bear aware:
   - Always carry bear spray on the trail. Make sure it's accessible and know how to use it. Bear spray is available in stores in towns throughout the Rockies. Staff are usually trained to teach you how to use it, so don't be afraid to ask for help! The Rockies are home to both grizzly and black bears, and you can run into them pretty much anywhere. They're not ubiquitous, but they are just as likely to show up close to town as in a berry patch next to a remote lake. Generally, bears avoid people, but encounters do occur. Avoiding this is your goal and this is what you should do:

- Make noise by calling out, clapping, singing, or talking loudly near streams, dense vegetation, and berry patches. Bear bells are NOT effective (and have even facetiously been referred to as dinner bells).
- Watch for fresh signs: Tracks, droppings (scat), diggings, torn-up logs, dead animals, and turned-over rocks are evidence of a bear in the area. Leave the area if these are new.
- Always keep your dog on a leash.
- Hike in a group of four or more.
- If you do encounter a bear, move away quietly if it hasn't yet seen you. If it's aware of you, stay calm and speak to the bear firmly to let it know you are human and not a prey animal. Back away slowly. Do not run!

2. Water is one of the most important things to bring on a hike. Two liters is fine for most hikes, but you may need more on hot days. If you have to use a natural water source, you should use a filter or iodine tablets to avoid waterborne parasites.

3. Be smart when you choose your clothing and always wear layers. On a tough climb you might feel warm in a t-shirt, but as soon as you stop at altitude you may need a down jacket, rain jacket, hat, and gloves.

4. Avalanches: You are visiting a cold mountain climate, which means there can be snow on the ground until late August. Make sure you check trail and avalanche conditions before heading out. (https://www.pc.gc.ca/en/voyage-travel/opv-tpt/sentiers-trails and https://www.avalanche.ca/en/map)

5. Bring snacks and/or lunch food with you and opt for meals that are high in protein. You'll need your energy and should be prepared in case you are on the trail longer than expected.

6. First Aid Kit: The smallest blister can ruin your day at the top of a mountain. Buy a kit or put one together yourself with medical tape, Band-Aids, alcohol wipes, tensors, antibiotic ointment, ibuprofen, and antihistamine tablets for bites and allergic reactions.

7. Carry a flashlight or headlamp as a contingency in case you are on the trail longer than expected.

8. Fire starter: Carry matches and/or a lighter in a waterproof container for emergency use, but inform yourself about fire regulations, bans, and the forest fire status and alerts.

9. Tools/equipment: Bring along a pocketknife or Swiss Army knife to help out in emergency situations; hiking poles for some of the steeper climbs; cleats or "spikes" for your shoes if there's partial or full snow coverage of the trail; and a whistle to alert others in case you need help.

10. Carry (and apply) insect repellent and sun protection. Mosquitoes can literally drive you crazy in the mountains.

11. Charge your phone and switch to airplane mode if using GPS (recommended) to save battery life. Bring a portable charger. Some hikes in the Rockies are out of cell phone range or have sporadic coverage. Familiarize yourself with the emergency SOS function on your phone.

HIKING SEASON

Most of the hikes in this book are best enjoyed from late April to October, but several are open year-round and can be done in proper winter hiking boots and spikes or crampons, or with snowshoes. Conditions vary and some trails are snowbound late into June and blanketed again in early October. June is the wettest month in the Rockies. To have the best chance of experiencing good weather, warmer temperatures, and easy access to subalpine hiking trails with meadows full of blooming wildflowers, head out in July and August. When planning your beer hiking journey, it's also worth keeping in mind that the larch and aspen trees will be turning gold in mid to late September. They offer a memorable backdrop to any hike and shouldn't be missed!

HUNTING SEASONS

Hunting seasons vary depending on the wildlife being hunted and the method of hunting. The archery-only season takes place on certain days between about August 25 and September 16, while the general (rifle) season runs from about September 17 to November 30 (also only on certain days). Hunting is prohibited on ecological reserves and in wilderness areas where wildlife is protected. In general, hunting and the discharging of firearms (and bow shooting) are prohibited in provincial parks and provincial recreation areas, but there are certain exceptions. To find out where hunting is permitted, visit https://albertaparks.ca/albertaparksca/visit-our-parks/activities/hunting/.

Here are some tips for staying safe when hiking in natural areas with wildlife:

- Be mindful: Recognize that hunting activities may be taking place in the area.
- Ensure you are wearing at least one article of clothing that is visible to hunters—clothes in hunter orange or another bright color.
- Alert hunters and wildlife of your presence by talking, whistling, or making noises.
- If you're visiting an area with your pet, ensure they are on a leash and are wearing something bright, such as a collar, leash, or clothing.
- Avoid hiking at dawn and dusk, and at any time when visibility is limited.
- Stay on designated trails and ensure you follow all signage.

WEATHER

It would be impossible to attribute one type of climate to the entire geographical region known as the Canadian Rockies as it's too large and diverse. The lowest recorded temperature in Banff, on the eastern side of the Rockies, was −51°F, while in the city of Nelson, which lies on the western side of the Rockies, the coldest temperature ever recorded was just –12.8°F. The mountains essentially make their own weather, which means it can be very location-specific and vary from one valley to the next. Even within a single day, temperatures and weather systems can change by the hour. In the winter, if a warm dry air mass (called a chinook) blows in from the west, temperatures can go from freezing to spring-like within hours. In the summer months, temperatures may hover around freezing during the night, even if the daytime temperature was in the upper twenties. The conclusion: When you're packing, be aware that you may experience what feels like all four seasons in a single day!

Website for local weather conditions: www.weather.gc.ca/canada_e.html

ADDITIONAL RESOURCES

GENERAL

Park passes for Canada: www.pc.gc.ca/en/voyage-travel/admission
Park passes must be purchased when entering individual national parks. The fee is $10.50 per person or $21 for a family or group. If traveling through several parks, a Parks Discovery Pass is recommended and can be purchased online at the address given above. The fee is $72.25 for an adult and $145.25 for a family or group.

Weekly bear report Banff, Yoho and Kootenay National Parks:
www.pc.gc.ca/en/pn-np/mtn/ours-bears/miseajour-update/miseajour-update-byk

ALBERTA HIKING RESOURCES

Hiking Alberta: www.travelalberta.com/ca/things-to-do/summer-outdoor-activities/hiking
Alberta trail reports and advisories: www.albertaparks.ca/albertaparksca/advisories-public-safety/trail-reports

ALBERTA BREWERIES

Alberta breweries: www.travelalberta.com/ca/places-to-go/road-trips/craftbeer-southern-alberta

ALBERTA VISITOR AMENITIES

Alberta provincial park passes: www.albertaparks.ca
Bear awareness: www.banff.ca/1009/Bear-Awareness
Wildfire status Alberta: www.wildfire.alberta.ca

BRITISH COLUMBIA HIKING RESOURCES

Hiking BC: www.bcparks.ca/recreation/hiking
BC trail reports and closures: www2.gov.bc.ca/gov/content/sports-culture/recreation/camping-hiking/sites-trails/alerts

BC BREWERIES

BC breweries: www.bcaletrail.ca/breweries

BC VISITOR AMENITIES

Wildfire status BC: www2.gov.bc.ca/gov/content/safety/wildfire-status/wildfire-situation

TRAIL ETIQUETTE

1. Share the trail: Many trails are for mixed use—hiking, horseback riding, and cycling. Cyclists and hikers yield to horses, and cyclists yield to hikers on most trails.

2. Leave no trace: Stay on the trail to protect valued plants and habitats. Also, make sure you always pack out what you pack in. And if you see an interesting stack of rocks, you've happened on a cairn. Cairns are there to help people find their way, so make sure you leave them undisturbed.

3. If hiking alone, make sure someone knows where you're going, when you'll be back, and what to do if you don't return on time.

Essentially, make yourself known, don't disturb wildlife, leave things the way you found them, and be mindful of trail conditions. Enjoying nature also means respecting your surroundings, so take your time and know your own limits.

MAP & INDEX

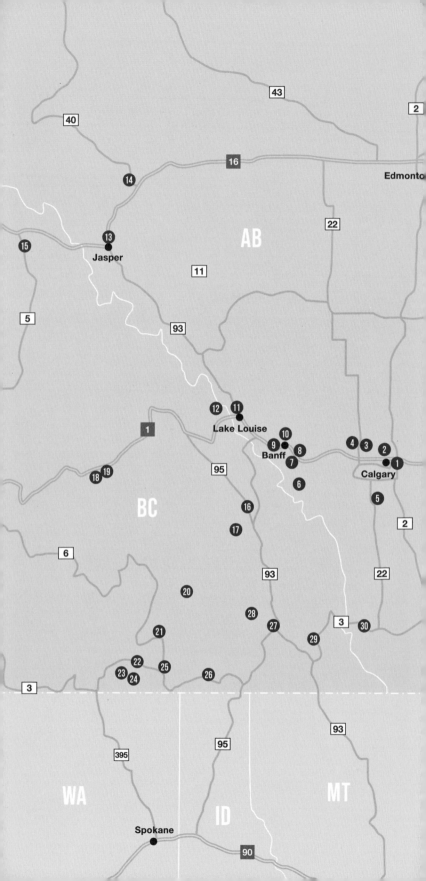

MAP

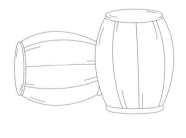

HIKES

NAME OF THE ROUTE	TOWN, PROVINCE, OR PARK	LENGTH	PAGE
Beaver Boardwalk	Hinton, AB	3.0 Km (Loop)	106
Begbie Falls	Revelstoke, BC	5.5 Km (Round-Trip)	130
Bighill Creek	Cochrane, AB	5.8 Km (Round-Trip)	48
Bow River Loop	Calgary, AB	8.2 Km (Round-Trip)	30
Creston Marsh Loop and a Wildlife Wander	Creston, BC	7.6 Km (Loop)	176
Delaurentiis Bluffs Lookout	Salmo, BC	6.1 Km (Round-Trip)	170
Elkhorn Cabin	Panorama,, BC	8.0 Km (Loop)	124
Emerald Basin	Yoho National Park, BC	10.3 Km (Round-Trip)	96
Friendship Trail	Black Diamond, AB	6.7 Km (Round-Trip)	52
Glenbow Trail	Rocky View County, AB	12.7 Km (Round-Trip)	42
Gorby Trail and Sherwoody Loop	Mount Fernie Provincial Park, BC	7.8 Km (Loop)	194
Ha Ling	Kananaskis Country, AB	7.0/7.8 Km (Round-Trip)	66
Hundred-Acre Wood Old-Growth Forest	Rossland, BC	3.0 Km (Lollipop Loop)	158
Juniper Trail	Radium Hot Springs, BC	7.2 Km (Loop)	118
Little Beehive	Lake Louise, AB	9.0 Km (Round-Trip)	90
Mel de Anna Trail Loop	Castelgar, BC	5.5 Km (Lollipop Loop)	152
Miral Heights and Bluffs Trail	Trail, BC	6.2 Km (Lollipop Loop)	164
Nose Hill Park	Calgary, AB	7.6 Km (Loop)	36
Policeman's Creek	Canmore, AB	4.8 Km (Loop)	72
Pulpit Rock	Nelson, BC	4.1 Km	148
Romantic Ridge	Kimberley, BC	6.3 Km (Loop)	188
Rummel Lake	Kananaskis Country, AB	11.3 Km (Round-Trip)	60
Spray River Loop	Banff National Park, AB	12.4 Km (Loop)	78
Stoke Climb	Revelstoke Mountain Resort, BC	14 Km (Round-Trip)	136
Swift Creek Loop	Valemount, BC	9.3 Km (Loop)	110
The Bee Line	Cranbrook, BC	4.8 Km (Lollipop Loop)	182
Turtle Mountain	Blairmore, AB	4.7 Km (Round-Trip)	200
Upper Kaslo River Trail	Kaslo, BC	7.0 Km (Loop)	142
Upper Stoney Trail	Banff, AB	4.0 Km (Loop)	84
Valley of the Five Lakes	Jasper National Park, AB	5.2 Km (Loop)	102

BREWERIES & BEERS

BREWERY	BEER	PAGE
Angry Hen Brewing Co.	Happy Pills European Pilsner	142
Arrowhead Brewing Company	Original '83 Honey Brown Ale	124
Banff Avenue Brewing Co.	Ride or Dry Pilsner	84
Cabin Brewing Company	Super Saturation New England Pale Ale	60
Canmore Brewing Company	Misty Mountain Hops New England IPA	66
Citizen Brewing Company	Wicklow Irish Stout	36
Cold Garden Beverage Company	The All-Nighter Vanilla Capuccino Porter	30
Erie Creek Brewing Company	Out Cold Cream Ale	170
Fahr Brewery	Bavarian-Style Hefeweizen	52
Fernie Brewing Company	What The Huck Huckleberry Wheat Ale	194
Fisher Peak Brewing Company	Hell Roaring Scottish Ale	182
Folding Mountain Brewing	Alpine Cranberry Sour	106
Half Hitch Brewery	Papa Bear Canadian Cereal Ale/Kölsch	42
Jasper Brewing Company	6060 Stout	102
Mt. Begbie Brewing Co.	High Country Kölsch	130
Nelson Brewing Company	Hooligan Pilsner	148
Over Time Beer Works	Split Wit Belgium White	188
Radium Brewing	Redstreak Red Ale	118
Rocky View Brewing Company	Rocky View Brown Ale	48
Rossland Beer Company	Rossland Genuine Draft American Lager	158
Rumpus Beer Company	Space Nugs Pale Ale	136
Sheepdog Brewing	Donnie G's Kölsch German-Style Lager	72
Tailout Brewing	Single Spey IPA	152
The Grizzly Paw/Chateau Lake Louise	Backcountry Blonde Ale	90
The Pass Beer Company	Copper Conductor Vienna-Style Lager	200
Three Bears Brewery	Happy Trails Pale Ale	78
Three Ranges Brewing Company	Ram's Head American Amber Ale	110
Trail Beer Refinery	Trail Ale American Red	164
Whitetooth Brewing Company	Whitetooth Session Ale	96
Wild North Brewing Company	Kootenay River Raspberry Sour	176

3

THE BEER HIKES

THE FOOTHILLS

BOW RIVER LOOP

RIVER WALK WITH EXCEPTIONAL VIEWS OF CALGARY

CALGARY
AB

▷⋯ STARTING POINT	⋯✗ DESTINATION
CONFLUENCE PLAZA, ST. PATRICK'S ISLAND	**PRINCE'S ISLAND PARK**
🍺 BREWERY	HIKE TYPE
COLD GARDEN BEVERAGE COMPANY	**EASY**
🐾 DOG FRIENDLY	📅 SEASON
YES (LEASH REQUIRED)	**YEAR-ROUND**
$ FEES	🕐 DURATION
$12/DAY FOR PARKING	**2–3 HOURS**
⛰ MAP REFERENCE	↦ LENGTH
CITY OF CALGARY	**8.2 KM (ROUND-TRIP)**
🔍 HIGHLIGHTS	〰 ELEVATION GAIN
CITY SKYLINE VIEW, TWO ISLANDS IN CITY'S CORE, ICONIC PEACE BRIDGE	**59 METERS**

THE ALL-NIGHTER VANILLA CAPUCCINO PORTER

5.8 % ALCOHOL CONTENT

 DARK EARTHY BROWN

 COFFEE, MALT, VANILLA, CHOCOLATE

 ESPRESSO, CHOCOLATE, VANILLA, EARTHY

BITTERNESS

SWEETNESS

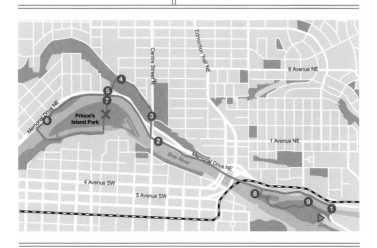

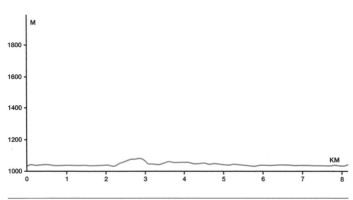

HIKE DESCRIPTION

Take an urban walk along a surging river, enjoy a panoramic view of the city, and stroll across a pair of delightful islands. Afterward, indulge in a smooth porter just minutes away in Calgary's historic brewing district.

The route begins on St. Patrick's Island, near the zoo, in Calgary's downtown core. Calgary is one of Canada's most populous cities, best known for its annual Calgary Stampede in July and for hosting the Winter Olympic Games in 1988. Historically, the city has been closely linked with oil exploration and cattle ranching.

As you begin the walk, you'll cross the Bow River on Baines Bridge before heading west along the north side of the river on the Bow River Pathway. You'll be near Memorial Drive, a major road that cuts through the city, but the paved pathway you'll follow is treelined and close to the Bow's shores. It's unlikely the route will be busy at this point, but you're bound to walk through flocks of Canada Geese nonchalantly claiming their territory while stand-up paddleboarders and rafters drift by on the water, doing what's popularly known as "Floating the Bow."

The pathway will lead you under Centre Street Bridge; here you'll cross Memorial Drive to access stairs that will take you to the pedestrian sidewalk on the bridge. At the end of the bridge, now on the north side of Memorial Drive, you'll take a right onto a smaller pathway that leads to Crescent Heights, where you can ascend McHugh Bluff to enjoy a stunning view of the city and of the Rocky Mountains on the western horizon. After a short walk on the bluff, a long set of wooden stairs will lead you back to the Bow River Pathway, which you'll continue heading west on until you reach the Peace Bridge, a candy-cane red, tubular construction that takes pedestrians and cyclists into the 20-hectare Prince's Island Park.

Our route walks the perimeter of the park, but you might feel inclined to drop into the island's interior to check out smaller pathways, water fountains, picnic areas, and the River Café restaurant—which happens to serve a selection of local craft beers. However, keep in mind that you have only just passed the halfway mark of this urban walk. Since the route ends minutes away from one of Calgary's oldest neighbourhoods (and what was historically referred to as Brewery Flats), you may want to hold out for a smooth dark Porter on the patio of Cold Garden Beverage Company.

Before long, you'll be cutting through Prince's Island Park to retrace your steps on the Bow River Pathway, then crossing a bridge onto St. Patrick's Island. Here you'll step onto more meandering paths and through naturalized wetlands where you might spot beavers and owls. Your route crosses the Island directly, taking you back to the parking lot. From here it's only a few minutes' drive to Inglewood and an energizing dark brew.

TURN-BY-TURN DIRECTIONS

1. From the parking lot, cross over the Bow River on Baines Bridge and turn left onto the Bow River Pathway, heading west. The path is also a bike path with periodic dual pathways for pedestrians.

2. At 2.0 km, pass under Centre Street Bridge and cross the eastbound lanes of Memorial Drive. Then turn left and walk 25 meters until you reach stairs leading up to the bridge.

3. At 2.4 km, turn left at end of the bridge on the path leading to Crescent Heights. Ascend to the bluff above the city.

4. At 3.0 km, descend to your left on wooden stairs and head toward Memorial Drive.

5. At 3.2 km, go right to cross the road on the overpass. At the end of the overpass, turn right on the Bow River Pathway, staying on the same side of the river.

6. At 4.2 km, turn left onto the Peace Bridge that leads to Prince's Island Park. Continue on the Bow River Pathway after crossing the bridge.

7. At 5.1 km, cross the Jaipur Bridge and turn right onto the Bow River Pathway heading east, in the opposite direction from which you came.

8. At 7.4 km, turn right onto the George C. King Bridge. Turn left immediately after the bridge, enter the park, and veer right on a paved path.

9. At 7.9 km, take a slight left at the fork and head straight through St. Patrick's Island toward the parking lot at Confluence Plaza.

FIND THE TRAILHEAD

The hike begins at the parking lot at Confluence Plaza on St. Patrick's Island at 1300 12 Street NE in Calgary. From downtown Calgary take the C Train to Bridgeland Memorial Station. You can begin the walk here by turning left on the Bow River Pathway, but the official trailhead (parking lot) lies 500 meters east. Get there by taking the Bow River Pathway to Baines Bridge on 12 Street NE/Zoo Road. Turn right onto the bridge and you will see the parking lot to your right.

COLD GARDEN BEVERAGE COMPANY

Located in Inglewood, which was historically the brewing district of Calgary, Cold Garden Beverage Company offers both a traditional and what it calls an "eccentric" line-up of beers. Its beers feature labels such as "Cakeface," "Red Smashed in Buffalo Jump," and "One Summer in Saskatoon." Its American Porter, brewed with cold press coffee and aptly named "The All-Nighter," will re-energize you after a long city walk in the sun. This chocolatey brew is the "favorite child" of Blake Belding, one of Cold Garden's owners. Inglewood was home to Alberta's first brewery, which produced its first batch in 1892 after prohibition was lifted—a full year before Calgary became a city.

LAND MANAGER

City of Calgary
City Hall and Municipal Complex
800 Macleod Trail SE
(403) 268-2489
www.calgary.ca

BREWERY/RESTAURANT

Cold Garden Beverage Company
1100 11 Street SE
Calgary, AB
T2G 4T3
(403) 764-2653
www.coldgarden.ca
Distance from trailhead: 1.2 kilometers

NOSE HILL PARK

GRASSLANDS GETAWAY IN SUBURBIA

CALGARY
AB

▷⋯ STARTING POINT	⋯✕ DESTINATION
NOSE HILL PARK 14TH STREET PARKING LOT	**NOSE HILL PARK PLATEAU**
🍺 BREWERY	🗺 HIKE TYPE
CITIZEN BREWING COMPANY	**EASY** 🚶
🐾 DOG FRIENDLY	📅 SEASON
YES (SOME OFF-LEASH AREAS)	**YEAR-ROUND**
$ FEES	🕐 DURATION
NONE	**2 HOURS**
⛰ MAP REFERENCE	↦ LENGTH
TRAILHEAD	**7.6 KM (LOOP)**
🔍 HIGHLIGHTS	〰 ELEVATION GAIN
INDIGENOUS MEDICINE WHEEL, THREATENED GRASSLAND ECOSYSTEM	**136 METERS**

5.2 %
ALCOHOL
CONTENT

WICKLOW IRISH STOUT

RICH BROWN

COFFEE,
CHOCOLATE,
GRAININESS

COFFEE,
BITTERSWEET CHOCOLATE,
CARAMEL

BITTERNESS

5
4
3
2
1

SWEETNESS

5
4
3
2
1

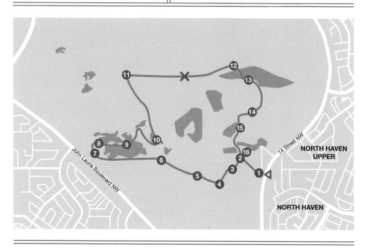

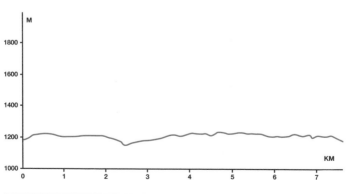

HIKE DESCRIPTION

Roam around a threatened ecosystem in one of Canada's largest urban parks; then walk or drive a few city blocks and treat yourself to a chocolatey stout.

At 11 square kilometers, Nose Hill Park, situated in the north-west corner of Calgary, is the fourth-largest urban park in Canada. It's home to a network of meandering trails (paved, gravel, and dirt) and a forested off-leash dog park. The route begins at the 14th Street lot in the park's southeast corner, which is one of six parking lots around Nose Hill's perimeter. Take a moment to enjoy a panoramic view of downtown Calgary from this prime vantage point before you head down into the prairie landscape.

From the trailhead, it's only a matter of minutes before you encounter one of Nose Hill's most interesting features, an authentic traditional medicine wheel built by the Blackfoot First Nations Tribe to maintain a spiritual connection to Na'a or "mother earth." The park is located on "Lookout Hill," or what the Siksikaitsitapi (Blackfoot Confederacy) call

Ootssapi'tomowa. Centuries ago, before Calgary was established, this was a sacred place for First Nations people who used the hill as a lookout spot. The Blackfoot prefer the term "sun wheel" to refer to this stone circle that's divided into four parts to signify the four Blackfoot nations. The four parts are also symbolic of the four cardinal directions, the four seasons, the four aspects of a person (physical, spiritual, mental, and emotional) and the four elements (fire, earth, wind, and water). Anyone can enter the circle to connect with the creator, but it's important to do so at one of the two gateways, which are located on the east and west sides, to move around the wheel in a clockwise direction and to leave using the same gateway.

Leaving the medicine wheel, you'll return to the path and immediately begin your trek westward through the grasslands. Nose Hill is one of the last remaining examples of the high plains that once covered this region. It is a Rough Fescue grassland ecosystem—one of the most threatened ecosystems in the world. As the sounds of the city fall away, the Rocky Mountains will begin to appear on the horizon to your left. Despite being about 80 kilometers away, the craggy peaks offer an impressive backdrop to your urban prairie walk.

As you near the park's western perimeter, you'll descend into Many Owls Valley before making your way up to the plateau on which you'll traverse the park toward the east. In the coulees and on the open prairie you might spot large mammals such as deer and coyotes, or come across porcupines, northern pocket gophers, ground squirrels, mice, and voles. In the grasslands, you'll find flora such as purple prairie crocuses and yellow buffalo bean, pink wild roses, orange lilies, and purple lupines.

As the path turns south, the city will come back into view, and you may see planes landing and taking off at Calgary's international airport. Winding your way back to the trailhead, you'll pass through the Big Rocks Viewpoint. The massive boulders here are an excellent place to take a rest, have a snack, and admire the panoramic view before walking the final ten minutes back to the trailhead.

TURN-BY-TURN DIRECTIONS

1. From the west end of the parking lot, take the paved uphill path toward the radio tower for 0.3 km and reach an intersection.
2. At the intersection at 0.3 km, turn left. Look out for the first of several rusty metal trail markers with flowers engraved on them.
3. At 0.5 km, arrive at the Indigenous medicine wheel.
4. At 0.9 km, go right on the gravel path.
5. At 1.1 km, continue straight ahead at the intersection. (There's a map at the intersection.)
6. At 1.5 km, go left at the fork.
7. At 2.4 km, turn right on the paved path.
8. At 2.5 km, turn right on the paved path.
9. At 2.9 km, the path forks onto a gravel path near a sign and a bench. Remain on the paved path.
10. At 3.5 km, continue straight on the paved path.
11. At 4.5 km, a paved path veers to the left. Turn right into the park interior on the wide grassy dirt path.
12. At 5.9 km, turn right at the metal trail marker.
13. At 6.1 km, reach an intersection at the top of the hill and go left on the gravel path.
14. At 6.4 km, reach the Big Rocks Viewpoint.
15. At 6.9 km, go left at the fork (after the benches). The radio tower is on the left.
16. At 7.4 km, reach the radio tower and turn left to return to the parking lot.

FIND THE TRAILHEAD

The parking lot is located at 64th Avenue and 14th Street. If taking public transit, take the number 20 bus to Nb 4th Street NW at 68th Avenue (Superstore) then walk to Sb 4th Street NW. At S of 72nd Avenue NW wait for the number 5 bus (North Haven) and take it to Wb Norfolk Drive at Theodore Place NW. Walk 340 meters to Nose Hill Park.

CITIZEN BREWING COMPANY

The owners of Citizen Brewing Company support initiatives to make the world a better place. Funds go toward such things as clean water initiatives, the Pink Boots Society (women beer professionals), LGBTQIA+ initiatives, and local programs and charities. The brewery also donates all spent grain to local biodynamic and small-scale animal farms, where it is used as feed. With a 50-seat taproom and a patio with room for over 200 (dogs welcome), the brewery prides itself on offering an inclusive space where everyone feels welcome. Kick off your boots and sit back with a velvety smooth Wicklow Nitro Stout. Its exceptionally thick, long-lasting foam and chocolatey taste will give you a boost after an afternoon spent wandering on the open prairie.

LAND MANAGER

Calgary Parks
City Hall and Municipal Complex
800 Macleod Trail SE
403 (268-2489)
www.calgary.ca

BREWERY/RESTAURANT

Citizen Brewing Company
227 35 Avenue NE
Calgary, AB
T2E 2K5
(403) 474-4677
www.citizenbrewingcompany.com
Distance from trailhead: 5 kilometers

GLENBOW TRAIL

A RIVER WALK WITH HISTORICAL HIGHLIGHTS

ROCKY VIEW COUNTY
AB

▷⋯ STARTING POINT	⋯✗ DESTINATION
GLENBOW RANCH PROVINICAL PARK	**MICHAEL'S CREEK**
🍺 BREWERY	卍 HIKE TYPE
HALF HITCH BREWING COMPANY	**EASY**
🐾 DOG FRIENDLY	📅 SEASON
YES (LEASH REQUIRED)	**YEAR-ROUND**
$ FEES	🕐 DURATION
NONE	**3 HOURS**
⛰ MAP REFERENCE	↦ LENGTH
AT THE TRAILHEAD	**12.7 KM (ROUND-TRIP)**
🔎 HIGHLIGHTS	〰 ELEVATION GAIN
THE GHOST TOWN OF GLENBOW, THE HISTORIC COCHRANE RANCHE	**178 METERS**

PAPA BEAR
CANADIAN CEREAL
ALE/KÖLSCH

 MEDIUM GOLD

 GRAIN,
GRASSY,
HINT OF LEMON

 PEPPERY,
HINT OF LEMON,
EARTHY

BITTERNESS

5
4
3
2
1

SWEETNESS

5
4
3
2
1

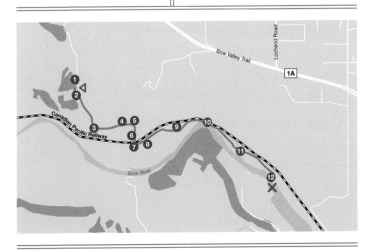

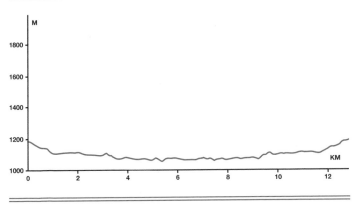

HIKE DESCRIPTION

A new provincial park offering an historically immersive experience in Alberta's rolling foothills will make you feel like you've stepped back in time and into the middle of nowhere. In fact, the town of Cochrane is only minutes away and a Papa Bear Kölsch is waiting for you on tap.

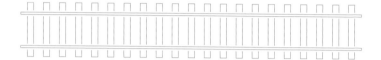

Less than an hour's drive from Calgary, Glenbow Ranch Provincial Park is one of Alberta's newest provincial parks, but the history of the region it's in runs deep. The park's 28-plus kilometers of pathways loop and meander through ravines where First Nations people once corralled bison and established tipi camps. Parts of the park used to be home to the historic Cochrane Ranche, which was Alberta's first large-scale cattle ranch and Western Canada's first government-lease ranch. The terms of the lease were a penny per acre per year. The park is also the site of the ghost town of Glenbow, a dynamic community in the early 1900s until the closure of its sandstone quarry and the subsequent cessation of its brickyards at the start of World War I. The last inhabitants moved away from these parts in 1927.

Just after leaving the parking lot, you'll pass a visitor center that includes an exhibit area highlighting the rich natural and cultural history of the Glenbow Valley. There is also information desk with very helpful staff. It's worth checking out!

On the Glenbow Trail, which drops down from the parking lot and snakes along close to the Bow River, you'll pass the remnants of a post office, a general store, and horse corrals—the ghost town of Glenbow. Interpretive signs along the way add depth to your walk through the park, providing information about the school that used to sit up on the hill and how the construction of the Canadian Pacific Railway (whose tracks you'll cross since it runs straight through the park) transformed the once-isolated community. Apart from the historical pageant surrounding you, this hike offers a scenic river walk through grasslands and woods with eye-catching views of aspen-speckled foothills and, beyond them, the Rockies. Keep an eye out, as you may even spot skittish whitetail deer and skulking coyotes. The Narrows, where you'll find yourself on a tree river flat full of trees, is an excellent spot for birdwatching. Spend time listening at the river's edge and you may hear pileated woodpeckers, kingbirds, and an assortment of songbirds.

TURN-BY-TURN DIRECTIONS

1. From the parking lot, head south into the park.
2. At 0.2 km, after the visitor center, go left to join the Glenbow Trail at the sign.
3. At 1.0 km, go left, staying on the Glenbow Trail.
4. At 1.7 km, pass the corrals.
5. At 2.0 km, turn right at the rest point to stay on the Glenbow Trail.
6. At 2.3 km, arrive at a viewpoint with a bench just before the railway tracks.
7. At 2.4 km, after crossing the tracks, follow the Glenbow Trail to the left and head east, parallel to the Bow River.
8. At 2.8 km, reach another rest point with picnic tables and toilets.
9. At 3.5 km, reach flats where the original Glenbow Village used to be.
10. At 4.4 km, reach a lookout point next to the Bow River.
11. At 5.2 km, come to "The Narrows" (treed river flats).
12. At 6.4 km, reach the turn-around point at Michael's Creek. Return the way you came.

FIND THE TRAILHEAD

From downtown Cochrane, head east on the Bow Valley Trail/AB-1A toward Centre Avenue. After 5.2 kilometers, turn right onto Glenbow Road AB-1A and continue for 2.8 kilometers. Turn right and pull up at the parking lot for Glenbow Ranch Provincial Park.

HALF HITCH BREWING COMPANY

Half Hitch Brewing Company is a family business run by siblings. It opened in 2016, a few years after the Haier/Kozloski family, swapping business ideas around the dinner table, agreed to start making beer. They developed a passion for the craft and with it a drive to create recipes and learn the ins and outs of the brewing process. If you line their four staple beers up in a row, the names and graphics portray an old western narrative that starts with a Papa Bear Kölsch and ends with a Shotgun Wedding brown ale, with a Farmer's Daughter pale ale and Fire n' Fury red ale between them. The Papa Bear brew was a gold-medal winner in the category of Canadian Cereal Ale at the 2018 Alberta Brewing Awards. The half-hitch? Well, that's just a knot used to tie your horse to a post while you go inside to cool down after a long day on the trail.

LAND MANAGER

Alberta Parks
9820 106 Street
Edmonton, AB
T5K 2J6
(877) 537-2757
www.albertaparks.ca

BREWERY

Half Hitch Brewing Company
10 Griffin Industrial Point 1
Cochrane, AB
T4C 0A2
(403) 988-4214
www.halfhitchbrewing.ca
Distance from trailhead: 10.2 kilometers

BIGHILL CREEK

A CREEK-SIDE WALK THROUGH A WILDLIFE RAVINE

COCHRANE
AB

▷⋯ STARTING POINT	⋯✕ DESTINATION
4TH AVENUE WEST, COCHRANE	**RAVINE VIEWPOINT**
🍺 BREWERY	🏁 HIKE TYPE
ROCKY VIEW BREWING COMPANY	**EASY** 🚶
🐾 DOG FRIENDLY	📅 SEASON
YES (LEASH REQUIRED)	**YEAR-ROUND**
$ FEES	🕐 DURATION
NONE	**1 HOUR 20 MIN.**
⛰ MAP REFERENCE	↦ LENGTH
ALBERTA PARKS	**5.8 KM (ROUND-TRIP)**
🔍 HIGHLIGHTS	〰 ELEVATION GAIN
A FIRST NATIONS BUFFALO JUMP, REMNANTS OF A FISH HATCHERY	**58 METERS**

ROCKY VIEW BROWN ALE

 DARK BROWN

 CHOCOLATE, MALT

 CHOCOLATEY

BITTERNESS

SWEETNESS

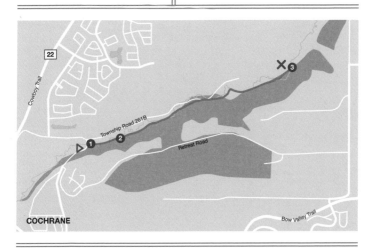

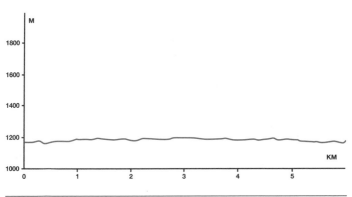

HIKE DESCRIPTION

Hike along a creek through a ravine carved out during the last ice-age. Post-hike, tip back an ale made with indigenous ingredients.

The Big Hill Springs Provincial Park is within Cochrane's city limits at the foothills of Alberta's Rocky Mountains. The park, an oasis amid a sea of urban development, is home to a tranquil ravine hike that passes by a series of small waterfalls glistening over rocky terraces. The Bighill Creek valley was carved out by meltwater during the end of the last ice age.

As you leave the parking lot, you'll see concrete blocks in the creek—remnants of a fish hatchery. Shortly afterward, you'll see another highlight: a buffalo jump used by First Nations peoples to hunt plains bison. The jump is on private property and may look like just another cliff, but archaeological work performed in the area has revealed bones and artifacts dating back to Indigenous encampments that are around 8,000 years old. Back then, the Kainai, Piikuni, Cree, and Tsuu T'ina stampeded buffalo between two barriers made of log and brush, forcing them toward a cliff or "jump." Before the introduction of horses, "buffalo runners," who were hunters dressed up as coyotes and wolves, would drive buffalo from grazing areas at full gallop towards the cliff, from which they would then plummet and either be killed in the fall or be massacred after.

The area around Bighill Creek is also a valuable wildlife corridor and provides a habitat for numerous species, from birds to bears; cougars and moose also frequent the area. Keep an eye out for poplar trees ready to topple over, their trunks chewed through by beavers, and nesting areas for great blue herons. The turn-around point is at the end of the trail. It's an open spot where you can look back and see down the whole ravine and even take in the peaks of the Rocky Mountains in the far-off distance. After doubling back, you'll emerge from the ravine. From here, it's a straight line downhill to Cochrane and the Rocky View Brewery where a chocolatey ale the color of a bison awaits you!

TURN-BY-TURN DIRECTIONS

1. Walk north from the parking area past posts with white and red markings and then past a green private property sign to access the trail.
2. At 0.4 km, the buffalo jump will become visible on the left.
3. At 3.0 km, reach the turn-around point. Return the way you came.

FIND THE TRAILHEAD

From Highway AB-1A E, which becomes the Bow Valley Trail as you near Cochrane, turn left on 4th Avenue N and continue straight for 1.4 kilometers. You'll drive directly into the parking lot, which is right by the trailhead.

ROCKY VIEW BREWING COMPANY

The Rocky View Brewing Company began as a nanobrewery in Bearspaw near Cochrane when Lyle Thorson, who was working an office job in Calgary, stoked his passion for home brewing on the weekends. In 2016, Lyle and his wife Denean Thorson transitioned the business into a fully operational brewery. In 2019, they expanded it to include a taproom and restaurant in downtown Cochrane. Their brown ale is part of their original range of beers that includes a witbier, a pilsner, a blonde, an amber, and an IPA. In celebration of Denean's Cree heritage, the brewery incorporates indigenous ingredients whenever possible. The brown ale uses honey from a Tsuut'ina Nation bee farm.

LAND MANAGER

Alberta Parks
9820 106 Street
Edmonton, AB
T5K 2J6
(877) 537-2757
www.albertaparks.ca

BREWERY

Rocky View Brewing Company
420 1st Street West
Cochrane, AB
T4C 1A5
(403) 851-1771
www.rockyviewbrewing.com
Distance from trailhead: 1.6 kilometers

FRIENDSHIP TRAIL

TWIN CITY CONNECTOR WALK IN ALBERTA'S WILD WEST

BLACK DIAMOND
AB

▷⋯ STARTING POINT	⋯✕ DESTINATION
SHEEP RIVER BRIDGE	**TURNER VALLEY**
🍺 BREWERY	🀰 HIKE TYPE
FAHR BREWERY	**EASY** 🚶
🐾 DOG FRIENDLY	📅 SEASON
YES (LEASH REQUIRED)	**YEAR-ROUND**
$ FEES	⏲ DURATION
NONE	**1 HOUR 30 MIN.**
⛰ MAP REFERENCE	↦ LENGTH
BLACK DIAMOND VISITOR MAP	**6.7 KM (ROUND-TRIP)**
🔎 HIGHLIGHTS	〰 ELEVATION GAIN
THE OLD MCPHERSON COAL MINE, PAINTED BIRDHOUSES	**58 METERS**

BAVARIAN-STYLE HEFEWEIZEN

 HAZY GOLD

 WHEAT,
WHITE PEPPER,
CLOVE

 WHEAT,
WHITE PEPPER,
BANANA

BITTERNESS   SWEETNESS

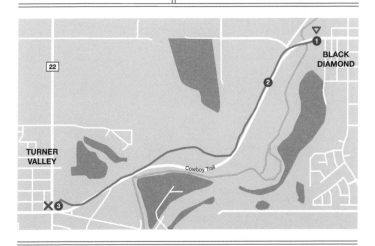

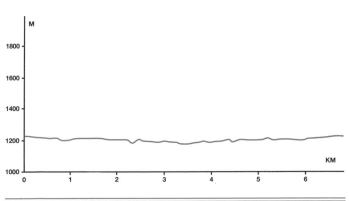

HIKE DESCRIPTION

Let your imagination take you back to the days of the wild west while walking along the Cowboy Trail in Alberta's Ranchlands. Then kick back and relax like a cattleman at the local watering hole to replenish after a day of exploring.

This semi-urban outing allows you explore two towns in Alberta's foothills in one afternoon by walking the Friendship Trail that connects Black Diamond and Turner Valley. The paved pathway runs parallel to Highway 22, also known as the Cowboy Trail. The two municipalities have existed as twin towns for years, but they united in early 2023 to become the entity now known as Diamond Valley. Black Diamond was

named for the coal deposits near the site of the original town. Turner Valley is known as the birthplace of Canada's petroleum industry and was named after Robert and John Turner, who settled in the area in 1886. Prior to this, the Blackfoot First Nations people inhabited the plains in this area of western Canada, where herds of wild wood bison roamed.

The trail features scenic viewpoints as well as the site of the old McPherson coal mine on the west bank of the Sheep River as you leave town. This outing in Alberta's Ranchlands is memorable, even in bad weather, and you can choose to lengthen your hike by exploring each of the two towns, visiting restaurants, boutiques, and, of course, craft breweries. You'll be walking beside sections of rocky hillsides that fall away on one side to reveal horse pastures, while an extended mountain view stretches out on the other side. Brightly painted handmade bird-houses decorate both sides of the pathway. This hike has the added appeal of a two-for-one brewery opportunity. You can walk straight to Fahr Brewery for a traditional Hefeweizen in Turner Valley and then, on your return to Black Diamond, head to the Hard Knox Brewery, adding another kilometer and a half to your trek. The Dusty Trail Ale awaiting you there will surely make it worth the effort!

TURN-BY-TURN DIRECTIONS

1. From the parking lot off Centre Avenue W, walk westward over the bridge until you see the sign for the Friendship Trail. Follow the trail until you reach Turner Valley.
2. At 0.8 km, there is a landmark rock on the other side of the highway. This is the site of the old Macpherson coal mine.
3. At 3.3 km, reach Millennium Park in Turner Valley. Return the way you came.

FIND THE TRAILHEAD

Drive west on Centre Avenue in Black Diamond (passing the large black diamond on your left). At the very edge of town, cross over Sheep River and turn right just after the bridge. The marked trail is immediately on your left; you'll see the path beside the highway you just turned off from. I recommend parking in the lot just before the bridge.

FAHR BREWERY

The mastermind behind Fahr Brewery is Jochen Fahr. Jochen was born and raised in Ebringen, Germany, close to where his father worked in a brewery. With Fahr Brewery, Jochen's goal is to provide the Canadian consumer with authentic German beer made from original German recipes. While earning a Bachelor of Engineering in biotechnology and a biomedical engineering PhD, Jochen kept his passion for beer alive by brewing at home. He even used his engineering skills and ingenuity to create his own automated brewing system, which has won him several medals in home-brewing competitions.

In 1516, Germany introduced laws stating that beer could only contain three ingredients: barley, hops, and water. This changed slightly in 1993, when yeast was added to the list. In 2015, when Fahr Brewery started full-time operations, Jochen promised to adhere to this latter standard. When visiting Fahr, why not start with the one that started it all—the Hefe—which was the first beer to be commercially produced by the brewery and was voted the best Hefeweizen in the world at the 2020 World Beer Awards!

LAND MANAGER

Town of Black Diamond
301 Centre Avenue West
Black Diamond, AB
T0L 0H0
(403) 933-4348
www.town.blackdiamond.ab.ca

BREWERY

Fahr Brewery
123 Kennedy Drive SE
Turner Valley, AB
T0L 2A0
(403) 800-6098
www.fahr.ca
Distance from trailhead: 500 meters

THE CENTRAL ROCKIES

RUMMEL LAKE

HIKE THROUGH A MOUNTAIN FOREST TO A LAKE

KANANASKIS
COUNTRY, AB

▷··· STARTING POINT	···✕ DESTINATION
MOUNT ENGADINE LODGE	RUMMEL LAKE
🍺 BREWERY	🔀 HIKE TYPE
CABIN BREWING COMPANY	**MODERATE** 🥾
🐾 DOG FRIENDLY	📅 SEASON
YES (LEASH REQUIRED)	YEAR-ROUND
💲 FEES	🕐 DURATION
YES	**3–4 HOURS**
⛰ MAP REFERENCE	↦ LENGTH
KANANASKIS COUNTRY	10.7 KM (ROUND-TRIP)
🔍 HIGHLIGHTS	⌇ ELEVATION GAIN
A MEANDERING CREEK AND A STRIKING MOUNTAIN LAKE	**419 METERS**

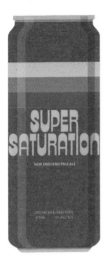

 6.0 %
ALCOHOL CONTENT

SUPER SATURATION NEW ENGLAND PALE ALE

 HAZY

 TROPICAL FRUIT,
PINE,
CITRUS

 SOFT,
JUICY,
FULL-BODIED

BITTERNESS	SWEETNESS

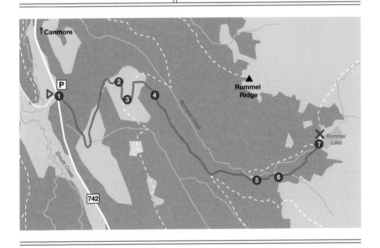

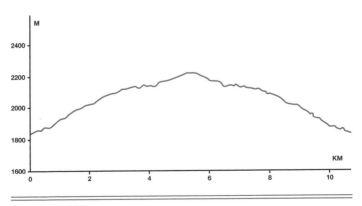

HIKE DESCRIPTION

Hike through a pleasant forest to stunning vistas and a spectacular mountain lake before chilling out with an NEIPA at a remote yet luxurious mountain lodge.

The remote Mount Engadine Lodge is located minutes from the Rummel Lake trailhead in the Spray Valley Provincial Park and about 45 minutes from the town of Canmore. This hidden gem brings luxury to the backcountry, providing overnight accommodations or temporary respite for hungry and thirsty hikers. The hike to Rummel Lake is a classic in "K-Country." If you visit the area in the fall, you'll be rewarded by the golden hue the larch trees take on as the weather turns cold. This trail is also a popular route for snowshoeing in the winter months.

From the trailhead, it's a moderate climb on a zigzagging, well-defined trail through the forest. As the trees thin, you'll get some lovely views back toward Tent Ridge and the Spray Lakes Reservoir before dropping into a mature forest. The trail meanders at an easy grade, occasionally even dipping down steeply as you make your way toward the lake.

Around 4.5 kilometers into the hike, you'll begin to hear Rummel Creek to your left. The trail is exceptionally narrow at one point as it meanders close to the creek. It's a good idea to take it slow here and be mindful

of your footing. You also have the option of heading left across a bridge at the 4.5-kilometer mark, instead of taking this more scenic but somewhat precarious section of the trail.

After walking for slightly less than 6 kilometers, you'll emerge from the woods on the shores of Rummel Lake. Named after Baroness Elizabeth (Lizzie) Rummel, a German-Canadian environmentalist and mountaineer, this classic Canadian mountain lake is nestled between Mt. Galatea and the Tower. You may want to walk along the lake's northern shore, with the option of continuing up another 3 kilometers to a valley that leads to Rummel Pass. This will add about another 2 hours to your adventure. If the lake is your final destination, the hike back along the same route is just as enjoyable as the journey in, but you now have a pint and a charcuterie board at the wonderful Mt. Engadine Lodge to look forward to at the end of it.

TURN-BY-TURN DIRECTIONS

1. The trailhead is an unmarked dirt path off the Smith-Dorrien Trail that begins just opposite Mount Shark Road.
2. At 1.7 km, reach a fine viewpoint.
3. At 2.0 km, arrive at another viewpoint with a bench.
4. At 2.3 km, reach a fork. Bear right, following the sign to Rummel Lake.
5. At 4.4 km, come to a lookout for Rummel Creek.
6. At 4.6 km, reach a fork and head right to take the more scenic (and trickier) route. Alternatively, stay left and follow the trail across the bridge.
7. At 5.4 km, arrive at Rummel Lake. Cross the creek over some logs to get to the lakeshore. Return the way you came.

FIND THE TRAILHEAD

To get to the Rummel Lake trailhead, head west from Canmore on the Smith-Dorrien Trail (Hwy 742) as it winds up into the Spray Valley. After 35.5 kilometers, turn right onto Mount Shark Road and you'll immediately see a sign for Mount Engadine Lodge. Park on the road to the Lodge just before or after the bridge crossing. Head back to Smith-Dorrien, where you'll see the unmarked trail heading southeast into the forest across the road. A conservation day-use pass is required to park your vehicle and can be purchased online for $15 per vehicle at www.conservationpass. alberta.ca/kcp.

CABIN BREWING COMPANY

The Cabin Brewing Company, which was chosen as Brewery of the Year at the 2020 Alberta Beer Awards, is based in the original "Brewery Flats" in far-off Calgary, but its beers are also available to quench your thirst in the Alberta backcountry. The humble cabin, according to the brewery's owners, "represents the ultimate escape." It is "a home away from home. A respite from the stresses of work and the regularity of everyday life. A place to be yourself." It's no coincidence, then, that Cabin's beer is served at the charming Mount Engadine Lodge, where it can be enjoyed on a terrace overlooking a meadow often grazed by moose. The property features a variety of accommodation options, including cabins, glamping tents, and rooms in the main lodge.

LAND MANAGER

Kananaskis Country Head Office
201 Railway Avenue
Canmore, AB
T1W 1P1
(403) 678-0760
www.kananaskis.com

BREWERY/RESTAURANT

Mount Engadine Lodge
1 Mount Shark Road
Canmore, AB
T1W 0B9
(587) 807-0570
www.mountengadine.com
Distance from trailhead: 260 meters

HA LING

A MOUNTAINEERING EXPERIENCE MINUTES FROM CANMORE

KANANSKIS COUNTRY, AB

▷··· STARTING POINT	···✕ DESTINATION
GOAT GREEK DAY-USE PARKING LOT	**HA LING PEAK (OR SADDLE)**
🍺 BREWERY	HIKE TYPE
CANMORE BREWING COMPANY	**STRENUOUS**
🐾 DOG FRIENDLY	📅 SEASON
YES (LEASH REQUIRED)	**YEAR-ROUND**
$ FEES	🕐 DURATION
A $15 CONSERVATION DAY-USE PASS IS REQUIRED TO PARK	**3–5 HOURS**
⛰ MAP REFERENCE	↦ LENGTH
KANANASKIS COUNTRY	7.0 TO SADDLE)/7.8 TO SUMMIT (ROUND-TRIP)
🔍 HIGHLIGHTS	〰 ELEVATION GAIN
EXCEPTIONAL RIDGE VIEWS, 360-DEGREE VIEW FROM THE SUMMIT	**748 METERS**

MISTY
MOUNTAIN HOPS
NEW ENGLAND IPA

6.4 % ALCOHOL CONTENT

 PALE,
HAZY,
STRAW

FRUITY,
CITRUS,
PINE

FRUITY,
LIGHT TART,
CITRUS

BITTERNESS

SWEETNESS

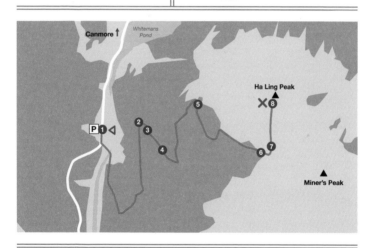

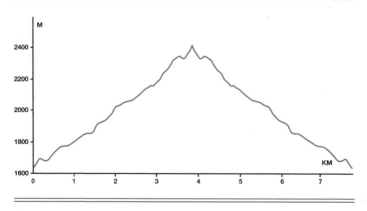

HIKE DESCRIPTION

Head out on a local out-and-back favorite with a steep ascent and the option of a summit scramble that will reward you with incredible views of the surrounding peaks. If a cloudy day in the Bow Valley interferes with your panoramic view, you can always nestle in with a Misty Mountain Hops to make up for it.

The small but bustling town of Canmore lies just a few kilometers east of Banff National Park. This mecca for outdoor enthusiasts sits nestled among the iconic Three Sisters and Ha Ling peaks. Ha Ling juts out from the northwestern end of Mount Lawrence Grassi, which is located just south of town.

The route up the northwestern slope of Ha Ling is a well-trafficked favorite of Canmore and Banff locals and is one of the most popular hikes in the Canadian Rockies. Just 15 minutes outside of town, this excursion will only take up part of your day but will give you a true taste of the rugged Rocky Mountain experience.

The ascent begins on meandering switchbacks through dense forest and doesn't let up. The steepness varies, and while this is not a technically difficult climb, it's a good idea to pace yourself early on. The trail has recently been worked on to make Ha Ling accessible for those who might otherwise have been intimidated by the elevation gain. Specifically, rails and cable ladders have been built for safety reasons and to ease the way up steeper sections. From the saddle at 3.5 kilometers, you can decide whether you want to climb another 400 meters to the Ha Ling summit or 300 meters in another direction to nearby Miner's Peak for a view of Ha Ling.

Most of the trail is extremely well maintained. Dirt and gravel paths alternate with steps carved into the rock (yeti steps). Higher up, at the treeline, three long wooden staircases have replaced steep switchbacks to ease the way onto the saddle. At the top of the stairs, you'll gain your first view over the upper ridge to the other side of the mountain. This breathtaking 360-degree vista is essentially the same as the one you'll experience from the summit, so if marching onward seems too difficult, or if the weather isn't cooperating, you may choose to turn around here. The view ranges from Goat Creek all the way to the Spray Lakes. To your right, Miner's Peak proudly juts out over Canmore, while to the left you'll have an up-close look at the southern summit of Mount Rundle. To the north, you can see from Mount Lady MacDonald all the way down the Bow Valley.

If you choose to summit Ha Ling, the final ascent is a bit of a scramble, with a multitude of trails traversing terrain consisting of loose rock and small boulders. Take your time and be mindful of your footing as you find the main arteries amongst the scree and boulders on the final 400-meter push to the summit. After that, it's all downhill as you zig-zag back to the base.

If you're an unexperienced hiker, you might not want to choose Ha Ling as your first winter hike. That said, it is a popular, well-trafficked route that is well maintained, even in winter. After summitting Ha Ling, you'll certainly have earned a cold IPA at the Canmore Brewing Company.

TURN-BY-TURN DIRECTIONS

1. From the parking lot, cross the Smith-Dorrien Trail and climb the embankment. Cross the bridge over the canal. You will see a sign that reads "Avalanche Hazard, Ha Ling Trail." Stay on the trail as you enter the forest.

2. At 1.5 km, flat-topped boulders offer a good first resting place in the summer.

3. At 1.6 km, you'll come upon the first chains and artificial footholds.

4. At 1.7 km, at a break in the trees, reach the first lookout point before continuing through the forest.

5. At 2.3 km, you'll come to a nice lookout point. This is a good spot for a rest and a good place to turn around if you don't want to go all the way to the summit.

6. At 3.3 km, you'll reach the treeline; after a traverse, climb the three separate wooden staircases.

7. At 3.5 km, reach the saddle.

8. At 3.9 km, arrive at the summit. Return the same way you came.

FIND THE TRAILHEAD

Ha Ling Peak Trail can be accessed via Spray Lakes Road (Hwy 742) above Canmore. At the turnoff to the Canmore Nordic Center, take the Smith-Dorrien Highway to the Goat Creek day-use parking lot. You will need to purchase a $15 pass to park, which you can get online at www.conservationpass.alberta.ca/kcp.

CANMORE BREWING COMPANY

The Canmore Brewing Company was founded by a couple of East Coast Canadian brothers. They now call the West, with its mountains and lakes, their "playground" and encourage everyone to "share times and stories with friends, family, and strangers over a beer." Along with its core beers, which include Misty Mountain Hops, the brewery serves seasonal brews, pilot brews (their latest small-batch creations), and beer cocktails. If their light fare doesn't satisfy your hunger after your long hike, you can order take-out from any Canmore restaurant and have it delivered to you at the brewery.

LAND MANAGER

Kananaskis Country Head Office
201 Railway Avenue
Canmore, AB
T1W 1P1
(403) 678-0760
www.kananaskis.com

BREWERY

Canmore Brewing Company
1460 Railway Avenue
Canmore, AB
T1W 1P6
(403) 678-0760
www.canmorebrewing.com
Distance from trailhead: 10.7 kilometers

POLICEMAN'S CREEK

AN EASY HIKE AROUND A PICTURESQUE MOUNTAIN TOWN

CANMORE
AB

▷··· STARTING POINT	···✕ DESTINATION
"BIG HEAD" SCULPTURE	ENGINE BRIDGE
🍺 BREWERY	🔀 HIKE TYPE
SHEEPDOG BREWING	**MODERATE** 🚶
🐾 DOG FRIENDLY	📅 SEASON
YES (LEASH REQUIRED)	YEAR-ROUND
$ FEES	🕐 DURATION
NONE	**1 HOUR 15 MIN.**
⛰ MAP REFERENCE	⊢ LENGTH
AT TRAILHEAD	**4.8 KM (LOOP)**
🔍 HIGHLIGHTS	〰 ELEVATION GAIN
ALAN HENDERSON'S "BIG HEAD" SCULPTURE, VIEWS OF THE THREE SISTERS PEAKS	**6 METERS**

DONNIE G'S KÖLSCH GERMAN-STYLE LAGER

4.4 %
ALCOHOL
CONTENT

 CLEAR, GOLDEN

 FRUITY, MALT

 BREADY, PEAR, CRISP

BITTERNESS

SWEETNESS

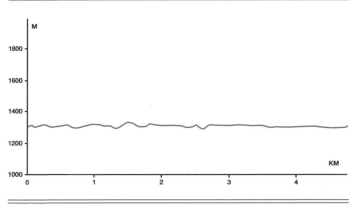

HIKE DESCRIPTION

Before sipping an exceptional Canmore Kölsch, soak up nature and history as you meander in and around a delightful mountain town.

This casual walking trail allows for a rich outdoor experience despite not straying too far from downtown Canmore. Nestled in the Bow Valley on the eastern edge of Banff National Park, Canmore is somewhat less touristy than Banff but just as charming. If you want to get a lay of the land and appreciate the natural beauty and history that surround the town without having to do any climbing, Canmore's Bow River Trail will delight.

Scottish workers arrived in Canmore to find employment at the coal mines in the late 1800s and Canmore was named shortly after by a Scotsman, Donald A. Smith, a high-ranking employee of the Canadian Pacific Railway. The Scots are the third largest ethnic group in Canada and were among the first Europeans to establish themselves in the country. Canmore is named after Ceannmore on the northwest shore of Scotland. In Gaelic, Ceannmore means "big head"; and nods to the town's Scottish heritage can be seen in its art, particularly in the over-sized cranium sculpture created by Alan Henderson that you'll encounter at the trailhead. From here, a gentle path will take you along a creek and through the trees to the Spur Line Trail, a piece of Canmore's coal-mining history. From the late 19th century to 1979, it served as a rail line for the mines.

The trail follows Policeman's Creek, a stream named after the N.W.M.P. barracks on its shores that were originally built in 1893 and that can still be visited today (they are mere steps from the trailhead). It passes over the Bow River via the historic Engine Bridge, which was built by the Canadian Pacific Railway in 1891 but became a pedestrian bridge after the mine closed in 1970. Now a popular spot among

tourists and wedding photographers, it's an excellent vantage point from which to view the gorgeous peaks called the Three Sisters. But many more places along the route are exceptionally scenic and beloved of photography enthusiasts. Despite being close to downtown Canmore, you might spot wildlife such as foxes, coyotes, skunks, and beavers here. And you never know—it's not uncommon to see elk, moose or even bears, so be prepared.

A wide, well-maintained path along the other side of the Bow leads back into downtown Canmore. This stretch takes you through the main shopping street of Canmore, where you can do a reconnaissance of the boutiques before arriving back at the Big Head. You may wish to end things here, to hit the shops or grab a cold Kölsch, but our route turns right at the Big Head and proceeds to the phenomenally beautiful boardwalk along Spring Creek. This short loop extends through a yellow marsh to another bridge that leads to a hotel and residential area before winding up back at, you guessed it, the Big Head! Time for a cold one!

TURN-BY-TURN DIRECTIONS

1. From the trailhead, immediately cross the bridge over Policeman's Creek and follow the path along the creek.
2. At 0.7 km, cross the road and continue on the Spur Line Trail—a paved path.
3. At 1.3 km, reach Engine Bridge, cross it, and head back toward downtown Canmore on a wide path.
4. At 3.5 km, back at the Big Head, turn right onto the boardwalk following the Spring Creek Path.
5. At 4.2 km, cross the bridge.
6. At 4.8 km, reach the head again.

FIND THE TRAILHEAD

The hike begins at the "Big Head" sculpture in the town of Canmore, where 8th Street meets Policeman's Creek, just past Spring Creek Drive. Parking can be found at 6th Avenue and 7th Street. From the parking lot, turn right on 8th and walk one block. The trailhead will be to your left. Alternatively, take the regional route 3 Roam Transit bus to Shopper's Drug Mart on Railway Avenue and 10th Street. From there, walk west on Railway Avenue to 8th Street and turn right. Walk to the bridge. The trailhead will be on your right.

SHEEPDOG BREWING

Sheepdog is a small-batch microbrewery on the outskirts of Canmore, Alberta. At the 2020 Alberta Beer Awards, it placed third in the New Brewery of the Year category. The owners say that in addition to producing a wide variety of beers for the taproom, brewing small batches keeps their creativity piqued. One owner is a firefighter, the other is in law enforcement, and the third is a veteran. The name Sheepdog refers to the protective function shared by these three jobs and the brewery has become a place for locals who look out for one another to gather: a "local hub" for first responders, veterans, and military personnel. Dogs are allowed both on the patio and in the taproom.

LAND MANAGER

Town of Canmore
Elevation Place
700 Railway Avenue
Canmore, AB
T1W 1P4
(403) 678-8920

BREWERY

Sheepdog Brewing
105 Bow Meadows Crescent Unit 112
Canmore, AB
T1W 2W8
(403) 679-4009
www.sheepdogbrewing.com
Distance from trailhead: 3.5 kilometers

SPRAY RIVER LOOP

FOLLOW A BUBBLING RIVER ON A FORESTED PATH NEAR DOWNTOWN BANFF

BANFF NATIONAL PARK, AB

▷··· STARTING POINT	···✕ DESTINATION
SPRAY WEST PARKING LOT	**GOAT CREEK BRIDGE**
🍺 BREWERY	🔁 HIKE TYPE
THREE BEARS BREWERY	**MODERATE**
🐾 DOG FRIENDLY	📅 SEASON
YES (LEASH REQUIRED)	**YEAR-ROUND**
$ FEES	🕐 DURATION
NONE	**3 H 30 MIN./5 H**
⛰ MAP REFERENCE	↦ LENGTH
AT TRAILHEAD	**12.4 KM (LOOP)**
🔍 HIGHLIGHTS	〜 ELEVATION GAIN
GRAND HOTEL, ROARING WATERFALL	**194 METERS**

5.0%
ALCOHOL CONTENT

HAPPY TRAILS PALE ALE

 AMBER

 LIGHT CITRUS, FLORAL

 HOP FORWARD, BREADY

BITTERNESS	SWEETNESS

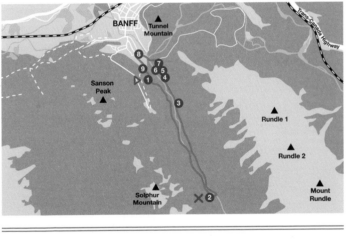

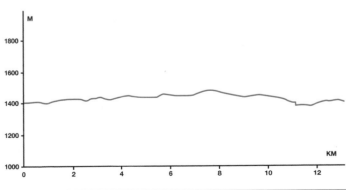

HIKE DESCRIPTION

Follow a rushing river that cuts through a thick forest minutes from the world-famous Fairmont Banff Springs Hotel. Afterward, reflect on your happy day on the trails with a pale ale that's just right at the three bears brewery.

If you're staying in the Town of Banff, don't miss out on the Spray River Loop, one of the most accessible hikes in the area. You'll begin about 100 meters from the majestic Fairmont Banff Spring Hotel on the town's southern boundary and immediately leave the crowds of tourists behind as you step onto the Spray River Fire Road and disappear into a thick forest. Named after the river surging nearby, the trail allows periodic glimpses of the water as you meander through the valley. The route provides views of all sides of the historic Banff Springs Hotel, which was opened in 1888 by the Canadian Pacific Railway.

As you make your way along the west side of the river, Mount Rundle is on your left and Sulphur Mountain rises to your right. It's a gentle walk on a relatively quiet route with the occasional uphill climb. The halfway point comes at Goat Creek Junction where you'll cross a bridge over Spray River before continuing back on the east side of the river. The trail is narrower this side as it leads back to the hotel via the Fairmont Banff Springs Hotel Golf course. Before looping around the hotel to return to the trailhead, you'll be treated with a visit to one of Banff's main attractions, the roaring Bow Falls.

TURN-BY-TURN DIRECTIONS

1. From the trail sign at the far end of the parking lot, head East on the fire road.
2. At 5.4 km, turn left at the junction onto the Spray Loop instead of continuing to follow Goat Creek Trail. Cross the bridge to the east side of Spray River.
3. At 9.3 km, there's a lookout point and view of the Banff Springs Hotel.
4. At 10.4 km, go right at the fork and walk along the boundary of the golf course on a dirt horse path.
5. At 10.5 km, turn left at the fork and cross Golf Course Road to take the horse path on your left.
6. At 10.8 km, cross the bridge and turn right onto the Bow Falls Trail.
7. At 11 km, reach the falls. From Cross Bow Falls Avenue, after the parking lot, turn right onto the horse path and continue uphill toward Spray Avenue.
8. 11.6 km, turn left onto Spray Avenue and walk toward the Fairmont Banff Springs Hotel.
9. At 12.0 km, continue to the opposite side of the roundabout and walk under the arch toward the parking lot and back to the trailhead.

FIND THE TRAILHEAD

Head south on Banff Avenue from the town of Banff and cross the Bow River Bridge. Turn left onto Spray Avenue. Once you reach the Fairmont Banff Springs Hotel, the road ends at a roundabout. Take the roundabout and immediately turn right, passing under an archway. Continue for 100 meters past the hotel parking and come to a parking lot for Spray River West.

THREE BEARS BREWERY AND RESTAURANT

The Three Bears offers beer hikers one of the most fitting beer drinking experiences in the Rockies. The all-in-one restaurant and brewery houses its fermentation tanks visibly in the back while surrounding guests with an outdoor mountain feel. With a retractable roof for star-gazing that opens up over tables surrounded by flora—and the odd Grizzly Bear and Mountain Lion—it's made an admirable effort to bring the outdoors inside. The Three Bears serves up the classics made with pure glacial water.

LAND MANAGER

Banff National Park (Parks Canada)
Banff Visitor Centre
224 Banff Avenue
Banff, AB
T1L 1B3
(403) 762-8421
www.pc.gc.ca/en/pn-np/ab/banff/info

BREWERY/RESTAURANT

Three Bears Brewery and Restaurant
205 Bear Street
Banff, AB
T1L 1A1
(403) 985-8038
www.threebearsbanff.com
Distance from trailhead: 2 kilometers

UPPER STONEY TRAIL

SUMMIT A MOUNTAIN MINUTES FROM THE TOWN OF BANFF

BANFF
AB

▷⋯ STARTING POINT	⋯✗ DESTINATION
MOUNT NORQUAY SKI AREA	**STONEY LOOKOUT**
🍺 BREWERY	🔳 HIKE TYPE
BANFF AVENUE BREWING CO.	**MODERATE** 🚶
🐾 DOG FRIENDLY	📅 SEASON
YES (LEASH REQUIRED)	**YEAR-ROUND**
$ FEES	🕐 DURATION
NATIONAL PARK ENTRANCE FEE	**1 HOUR 30 MIN.**
⚠ MAP REFERENCE	↦ LENGTH
AT TRAILHEAD	**4.1 KM (LOOP)**
🔍 HIGHLIGHTS	〜 ELEVATION GAIN
MOUNTAIN VIEWS, ADJACENT TO SKI RESORT	**240 METERS**

RIDE OR DRY
PILSNER

 LIGHT AND CLEAR

 DRY WHITE WINE, CRISP

 DRY WHITE WINE, COMPLEX, LIGHT, CRISP

BITTERNESS   SWEETNESS

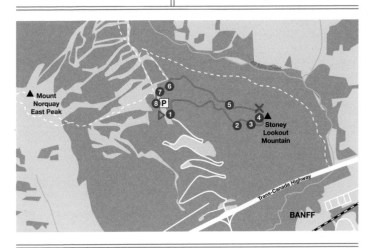

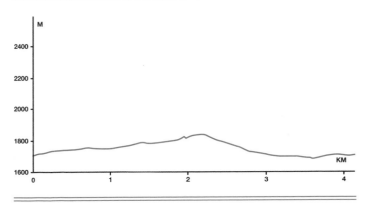

HIKE DESCRIPTION

Enjoy a short undulating loop through a fairy-tale forest with an outstanding viewpoint overlooking the town of Banff and the surrounding Bow Valley. Post-hike, replenish immediately with Banff Ave Brewing Co.'s Ride or Dry Pilsner, on tap at Mount Norquay's Cascade Lodge.

The picture-perfect town of Banff, situated in Canada's oldest national park, is a mecca for tourists and outdoor adventurers. Whether you are strolling down the town's main street or exploring the rugged back-country, the scenery is guaranteed to dazzle. Upper Stoney Trail, while conveniently located close to town, is far enough removed from the congested streets to provide hikers with a true wilderness experience.

Our route, also known as the Stoney Lookout Loop, meanders up the spine of "Stoney," a promontory extending east from the slopes of Mount Norquay. The extensive overstory of the forest of lodgepole pines and spruces gives this hike a mystical feeling; beards of lichen hang from branches and moss blankets the ground throughout. Some parts of the trail are quite steep, but it levels off often enough for you to catch your breath.

This well-maintained, moderately trafficked trail can be enjoyed year-round. In the summer months there are many exposed roots, and the trail can be slippery after rainfall, so watch your step! During the winter, micro-spikes are a big help, as the entire trail is usually snow-covered and well-packed. When the snow is fresh this becomes a popular snowshoe route, so if the conditions are right, you might want to rent a pair from one of the numerous sporting goods stores in town.

As you approach the lookout at the loop's halfway point, the trail breaks out of the forest the town of Banff becomes visible below and a view of Bow Valley opens up to the west. Continuing briefly through the trees,

you'll reach the high point, Stoney Lookout, at a break in the forest with a phenomenal point-blank view of the iconic Cascade Mountain. Stoney itself was previously referred to as Stoney Squaw, a name that was removed from signage on the trail in 2020 due to the name's derogatory connotations. Cascade is the highest mountain adjacent to the town and is also known as Stoney Chief.

From the lookout, the trail twists mostly downhill through the forest and offers intermittent views of the Mount Norquay Ski Area. A short while later, you'll arrive at an intersection and turn left to follow the trail that takes you to the ski lodge. Here you might see mountain bikers shredding by, making their way to Lower Stoney Trail—a bike route that ends on the highway below.

Within minutes you'll be standing opposite the North American Chair, one of the continent's oldest lifts servicing some of its steepest ski runs. Below will be the rooftop of the ski lodge in which you'll make your final ascent: up the stairs to the Lone Pine Lounge, where you can wet your whistle with some of Banff Avenue Brewing Company's Ride or Dry. Alternatively, if you feel like you haven't yet been up high enough, you may choose to take a ride up the chairlift to the Cliff House Bistro for a pint and a panoramic view of Banff and all its surrounding peaks.

TURN-BY-TURN DIRECTIONS

1. A large green wooden sign (featuring a map) at the trailhead will direct you to the right, toward "Stoney Lookout." Almost immediately, another green sign reading "Stoney Lookout" will lead you onto the "Upper Stoney Trail". Follow this into the woods.
2. At 1.5 km, stay left at two consecutive brown and yellow directional hiking signs, making sure to descend on the main trail (unmarked).
3. At 1.8 km, clearings begin to appear in the trees and the first views of the valley below open up.
4. At 2.0 km, reach the high point, Stoney Lookout.
5. At 2.6 km, enjoy the first view of Mount Norquay Ski area through the trees.
6. At 3.8 km, come to a T-junction. There will be a green sign pointing toward the Mount Norquay Parking Lot. Turn left onto Lower Stoney Trail and head toward the Mount Norquay Ski Lodge.
7. At 4.0 km, begin descending down to the lodge on an old ski run (not a single-track path).
8. The parking lot is on the left just before the lodge.

FIND THE TRAILHEAD

From Banff, head northwest on Mount Norquay Road toward the Trans-Canada Highway. Remain on Mount Norquay Road past the turnoff to the highway; from here, 6 kilometers of switchbacks on a scenic paved road will take you directly to the resort parking lot. Immediately to your right will be a sign that reads "Stoney Lookout," marking the trailhead of the Upper Stoney Trail.

BANFF AVENUE BREWING CO.

Banff Avenue Brewing Co. was founded in 2010 and has developed into a beer-culture hotbed for locals and tourists alike. The Brewpub, as it's referred to by locals, is located in Banff's Austrian-inspired Clock Tower Mall. It draws on the strength of the dynamic Banff community (it brews an annual "Spirit of Norquay" beer) and the inventiveness inspired by the rugged mountains, wildlife, and nature that surrounds it. It will also, on occasion, incorporate unique tea blends from another locally owned store, the Banff Tea Company, into its feature beers to make an extra special brew. If you're looking for something that's always on the menu, take a walk on the wild side with the Ride or Dry Pilsner. Hopped with Nelson Sauvin hops to create a flavorful and unique white grape character, it's sure to become a fast favorite.

LAND MANAGER

Banff National Park (Parks Canada)
Banff Visitor Centre
224 Banff Avenue
Banff, AB
T1L 1B3
(403) 762-1550
www.pc.gc.ca/en/pn-np/ab/banff/info

BREWERY/RESTAURANT

Lone Pine Lounge
Cascade Lodge
Mount Norquay Ski Area
2 Mount Norquay Road
Banff, AB
T1L 1B4
(403) 762-4421
www.banffnorquay.com
Distance from trailhead: 550 meters

LITTLE BEEHIVE

HIKE FROM LAKE LOUISE TO AN ICONIC LOOKOUT

LAKE LOUISE
AB

▷··· STARTING POINT	···✕ DESTINATION
FAIRMONT CHATEAU LAKE LOUISE	**LITTLE BEEHIVE**
🍺 BREWERY	🏁 HIKE TYPE
THE GRIZZLY PAW/ CHATEAU LAKE LOUISE	**MODERATELY CHALLENGING**
🐾 DOG FRIENDLY	📅 SEASON
YES (LEASH REQUIRED)	**YEAR-ROUND**
$ FEES	🕐 DURATION
YES (PARKING $12.25/DAY)	**3 HOURS 30 MIN.**
⛰ MAP REFERENCE	↦ LENGTH
PARKS CANADA, LAKE LOUISE, AND MORAINE LAKE	**9.0 KM (ROUND-TRIP)**
🔍 HIGHLIGHTS	〰 ELEVATION GAIN
19TH-CENTURY GRAND HOTEL, MOUNTAIN LAKE, TEAHOUSE	**535 METERS**

BACKCOUNTRY
BLONDE ALE

GOLDEN

SWEET MALTS

MALTY,
LOW CARAMEL NOTES

BITTERNESS	SWEETNESS

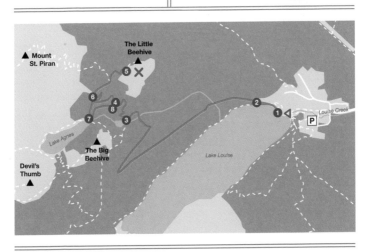

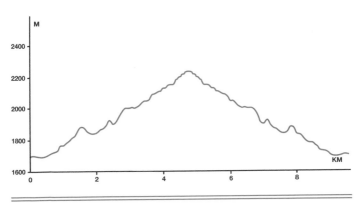

HIKE DESCRIPTION

 Venture out on an impressive out-and-back trail that begins at a World Heritage Site and features three lakes, a waterfall, and a stunning view. Quench your thirst immediately afterward steps from the lake's promenade with an ale brewed exclusively for the Fairmont Chateau Lake Louise.

Lake Louise has three parts: the townsite, the iconic turquoise green lake that sits on a plateau above it, and the world-famous ski area. The lake was originally known to the local Stoney-Nakoda people as "Ho-run-num-nay," or the "Lake of Little Fishes." The Little Beehive hike begins at the majestic Fairmont Chateau Lake Louise and is a local favorite. Known as "The Diamond in the Wilderness," the Chateau was built beginning in 1890 as part of the Canadian Pacific Railway's network of hotels. Walking along the paved walkway on the lake's eastern shore, it's easy to feel like you have entered a postcard. Victoria Glacier makes a beautiful backdrop, and its run-off feeds the aquamarine lake, dotted with red canoes, before you. Resist any temptation you may feel to spend your time here, because ahead of you lies the promise of one of the most epic views in the Rockies. Keep going!

From the lake's northwestern shore, you'll enter the woods and begin ascending a moderate incline on a wide dirt path. For the first couple of kilometers, you'll catch occasional views of Lake Louise through breaks in the trees. The trail then snakes deep into a spruce-and-fir forest on long switchbacks, but it won't be long before you begin to see more of the surrounding mountains. Fairholm Mountain will soon loom on your left. Some stretches of the trail are moderately steep with exposed roots and rocks, and it can be slippery depending on the season, so watch your step! The path will then lead you straight to the next body of water—Mirror Lake. Big Beehive, a small mountain resembling an enormous beehive, rises up on the opposite shore of the mountain lake, casting its reflection across its surface.

This is a perfect place to pause for a break on one of the benches and admire the tranquility of this quaint little lake. As you depart, leave on the lake's righthand side and head in the direction of Lake Agnes. You'll begin ascending on short switchbacks, gaining elevation quickly. The trail at this point is well maintained but rocky in places. A kilometer after Mirror Lake, you'll be offered a choice between going left, toward the Lake Agnes Tea House, or right, up to Little Beehive. This junction is the beginning of a loop, so whichever way you choose, you'll eventually end up at both Little Beehive and the teahouse. We suggest heading directly to Little Beehive and saving the busy teahouse for later. Switchbacks, and a moderate climb of about 20 minutes will bring you to the summit. You'll be greeted by a dizzying view of both the Chateau and Lake Louise from a standpoint 535 meters higher than when you began the hike. Several smaller trails surround this point of the trail, allowing you to appreciate the panoramic view of the Bow Valley from several vantage points. From this height, the hypnotic blue hue of the water dazzles, so find yourself a rock to perch on while you soak up the view.

Descending, retrace your steps to the first intersection, this time detouring 600 meters to see the scenic Lake Agnes and the teahouse that sits on its shores. The original teahouse, which was built in 1901 (and replaced in 1981), is said to have been the oldest in Canada. It was named after the original First Lady of Canada, Lady Agnes Macdonald, the wife of Canada's first Prime Minister, Sir John A. Macdonald. The Lake Agnes Teahouse is a notoriously busy spot so keep the chilled brew that awaits you below in mind if the line for a hot tea and cakes is too much to endure! Beneath the teahouse, a wooden staircase returns you to the trail that leads back to Lake Louise, but not before providing the rare opportunity of standing next to a raucous rocky mountain waterfall. Crowds can accumulate in this small area, so watch your step!

TURN-BY-TURN DIRECTIONS

1. From Chateau Lake Louise, walk 200 meters toward the Lake's northwestern shore.
2. Turn right at the sign reading "Lake Agnes Tea House and Big Beehive," and follow the trail.
3. At 2.7 km, as you arrive at Mirror Lake, follow the direction indicated by the sign for "Lake Agnes/Little Beehive."
4. At 3.3 km, turn right onto a trail that leads toward Little Beehive. There is no signage. Stay on the trail as it veers left.
5. At 4.4 km, reach the summit of Little Beehive. Descend from the summit in the direction of Lake Agnes.
6. At 5.0 km, continue toward Lake Agnes instead of rejoining the trail on which you came.
7. After about 500 meters, arrive at the Lake Agnes Tea House. Descend the stairs below the teahouse to reach the waterfall lookout.
8. At 5.6 km, continue straight at the fork (veering right) to return to Lake Louise.

FIND THE TRAILHEAD

Follow Lake Louise Drive from the village of Lake Louise to the Fairmont Chateau Lake Louise. Try to arrive early to find parking, or, to avoid the sure-to-be-full lot, take advantage of the "park and ride" shuttles run by Parks Canada from mid-May to mid-October from the Lake Louise ski area. The town of Banff also offers a year-round bus service from Banff to the lakeshore. From the Chateau, head northwest on a paved promenade along the lake for approximately 200 meters to get to the trailhead. There will be a brown and yellow sign listing several hikes, including the one to "Lake Agnes Tea House."

THE GRIZZLY PAW BREWING COMPANY

In collaboration with the Fairmont Chateau Lake Louise, The Grizzly Paw Brewing Company has created an ale that is exclusively available at the hotel. The proprietary brew, an ale called Backcountry Blonde, can be ordered in most restaurants and bars at the Chateau. The Fairview Bar and Restaurant is the perfect place to order this unique brew because of its magnificent view of Lake Louise. The Grizzly Paw's timber-framed brewery can be found in the town of Canmore, Alberta, which is 80 kilometers east of Lake Louise. Building on the success of their destination brewpub, which opened in 1996 in downtown Canmore, the owners of the Grizzly Paw opened three new establishments in the town. Each can of its Summit Series features beers named for mountains from the surrounding region. The range includes its Rundlestone Session Ale, Three Sisters Pale Ale, and Evolution IPA. If you enjoyed your Backcountry Blonde at Lake Louise, a scenic drive to Canmore and one of the Grizzly Paw's locations will be well worth the trip!

LAND MANAGER

Banff National Park (Parks Canada)
Lake Louise Visitor Centre
Samson Mall
201 Village Road
Lake Louise, AB
T0L 1E0
(403) 762-8421
www.banfflakelouise.com

RESTAURANT

Fairview Bar & Restaurant
Fairmont Château Lake Louise
111 Lake Louise Drive
Lake Louise, AB
T0L 1E0
(403) 522-1817
www.fairviewbar.com
Distance from trailhead: 200 meters

BREWERY

The Grizzly Paw Brewpub
622 Main Street
Canmore, AB
T1W 2B5
(403) 678-9983
www.thegrizzlypaw.com

EMERALD BASIN

CIRCLE A MOUNTAIN LAKE AND ASCEND TO ITS GLACIAL SOURCE

YOHO NATIONAL PARK, BC

▷··· STARTING POINT	···✗ DESTINATION
EMERALD LAKE LODGE	**EMERALD BASIN**
🍺 BREWERY	🗺 HIKE TYPE
WHITETOOTH BREWING COMPANY	**MODERATE**
🐾 DOG FRIENDLY	📅 SEASON
YES (LEASH REQUIRED)	**JULY–OCTOBER**
$ FEES	🕐 DURATION
NATIONAL PARK ENTRANCE FEE AND $6 PARKING FEE	**3 HOURS**
⛰ MAP REFERENCE	⊢ LENGTH
PARKS CANADA, YOHO NATIONAL PARK	**10.3 KM (ROUND-TRIP)**
🔍 HIGHLIGHTS	〰 ELEVATION GAIN
GLACIAL RUN-OFF LAKE, VIEWS OF SNOW-PEAKED MOUNTAINS	**242 METERS**

WHITETOOTH
SESSION ALE

GOLD	

SWEET MALT,
LIGHT MANDARIN
ORANGE

CRISP,
LIGHT,
GRAINY

BITTERNESS

SWEETNESS

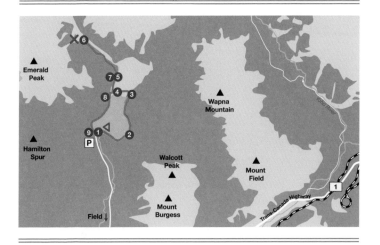

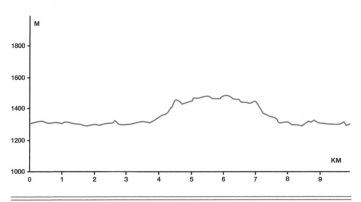

HIKE DESCRIPTION

Hike to a jewel of a lake and an avalanche-scoured basin surrounded by waterfalls and majestic peaks. Cool off at trail's end with a Whitetooth session ale on a lakeside patio.

Avoid the crowds common at the more well-known destinations in the Banff/Lake Louise area by driving a bit further down the Trans-Canada Highway and across the border into British Columbia to beautiful Emerald Lake. This dazzling destination lies in Yoho National Park. The name Yoho comes from a Cree expression meaning "awe and wonder." The first non-Indigenous person to set eyes on the lake was Canadian Pacific Railway (CPR) surveyor Tom Wilson, who accidently stumbled upon it in 1882 while tracking runaway horses.

Like Lake Louise, Emerald is an example of a glacial run-off lake. The name is an "on the nose" description of the color of this stunning mountain lake, which is generally frozen from November to late April. The charming Emerald Lake Lodge and its surrounding cabins sit on a peninsula on the lake's shore; here, our hike begins. Essentially, you'll be walking a counterclockwise loop around the lake with a diversion at the back end to undertake an out-and-back climb to Emerald Basin.

From Emerald Lake Lodge, proceed on a narrow dirt path on the lake's southeast shore. Even in mid-summer, this path can be wet, muddy, and slippery, so poles and waterproof footwear are a good idea. The region's climate is an anomaly in the Canadian Rockies. The basin traps moisture that, combined with the high elevation, produces a unique microclimate that looks and feels more like something you would experience on Canada's more humid West Coast. As you hike, you'll not only be treated to magnificent lakeshore views but also greeted by western red cedars, western yew, western hemlock, and western white pine, along with an abundance of berries and wildflowers. Be on the lookout for the occasional moose, bald eagle, or osprey as you head toward the lake's back end.

A short wooden bridge will take you onto a glacial outwash plain where the vegetation is thinner and crisscrossing streams meander from the glacier to the lake. As you approach a viewpoint with benches, a sign reading "Emerald Basin" will direct you onto a trail on which you'll begin the far less crowded hike to your destination. The trail here is wide and gentle, passing through cedars and fir trees. You'll see Michael's Peak rising up before you as you approach another sign for "Emerald Basin"; turning left, you'll begin a steep ascent on a narrow path through scattered pine trees. In the distance, you'll hear Emerald Creek rushing off to your right. The uphill push is quite steep, but it doesn't last for long. Soon the trail levels off, undulating closer to the ridge as the creek comes into view below. As you emerge above the tree line, the view expands to encompass the impressive President and Vice President mountains (named after the President and Vice President of the coast-to-coast Canadian Pacific Railway) rimming the basin before you. The trail disappears as you step into the belly of the basin (either onto a rocky floor or a snowy icefield, depending on the month you visit). The views south to Mount Burgess, Mount Stephen, Wapta Mountain, and Mount Field are incredible.

From Emerald Basin, retrace your steps to the lake. When you reach the shore, turn right to complete the loop around it. As you near Emerald Lake Lodge, there is an excellent lakeshore viewpoint toward the Burgess Shale, famous for its fossils that provide the oldest evidence of complex life on Earth. Continue left, across the bridge, to Cilantro Cafe to refresh yourself with an enticing session ale!

TURN-BY-TURN DIRECTIONS

1. From the parking lot, cross the bridge toward Emerald Lake Lodge, following the paved road through the cabins until it leads to narrow dirt path. There is no trailhead sign.
2. At 1.2 km, reach a sign reading "Burgess Pass." Stay left on the path as it circles the lake.
3. At 2.7 km, cross the creek over a wooden bridge.
4. At 3.2 km, rest at the wooden benches and take in view of the lake. Follow the sign on the right side of the trail pointing toward Emerald Basin.
5. At 4.0 km, a sign for Emerald Basin directs you onto another trail on the left.
6. At 6.0 km, reach the turn-around point in Emerald Basin and head back the way you came.
7. At 7.8 km, turn right at the sign for Emerald Basin.
8. At 8.5 km, reach the lake and turn right to round its other shore.
9. At 10.0 km, finish the hike at the picnic tables next to the lake, where you can enjoy a view of the Burgess Shale. From here, it's 250 meters to the parking lot.

FIND THE TRAILHEAD

Emerald Lake is near the town of Field in British Columbia, 50 kilometers from Lake Louise in Alberta and 93 kilometers from Banff. Head west from Lake Louise through Kicking Horse Pass. A kilometer west of Field, take the turnoff to Emerald Lake/Yoho National Park. The lake and its parking lot are a further 8.0 kilometers along, at the end of the road. Proceed across the bridge toward Emerald Lodge and walk on the paved path through the buildings until you come to the trailhead. The trail is unmarked but unmistakable.

WHITETOOTH BREWING COMPANY

Where the Rocky Mountains meet the Purcell Range in southeastern British Columbia lies the town of Golden, the home of the Whitetooth Brewing Co. Surrounded by five national parks—Yoho, Banff, Jasper, Glacier, and Kootenay—this mountain town is another playground for you to discover in the wilds of the Rockies. The brewery is the community's first and opened in 2016 with the goal of "combining the best experiences that our expansive mountain playground has to offer with the perfect beverage afterwards." About halfway between Banff and Golden, the restaurants at Emerald Lake Lodge serve a selection of Whitetooth's beers. Perched on a peninsula on Emerald Lake, Cilantro Café's patio is an idyllic spot to refuel with casual Rocky-Mountain cuisine and a refreshing session ale. The Whitetooth Session Ale placed third in the North American Light Ale category at the 2022 BC Beer Awards.

LAND MANAGER

Yoho National Park (Parks Canada)
Yoho National Park Visitor Centre
5764 Trans-Canada Highway
Field, BC
V0A 1G0
(250) 343-6783
www.parks.canada.ca/pn-np/bc/yoho/visit/heures-hours

BREWERY RESTAURANT

Cilantro Café
1 Emerald Lake Road
Field, BC
V0A 1GO
(250) 343-6321
www.crmr.com/resorts/emerald-lake
Distance from trailhead: 200 meters

VALLEY OF THE FIVE LAKES

A CIRCUIT AROUND FIVE MESMERIZING LAKES

JASPER NATIONAL PARK, AB

▷··· STARTING POINT	···✕ DESTINATION
ICEFIELDS PARKWAY	**LAKE FIVE**
🍺 BREWERY	🗺 HIKE TYPE
JASPER BREWING COMPANY	**MODERATE** 🚶
🐾 DOG FRIENDLY	📅 SEASON
YES (LEASH REQUIRED)	**YEAR-ROUND**
$ FEES	🕐 DURATION
NATIONAL PARK ENTRANCE FEE	**1 HOUR 30 MIN.**
⛰ MAP REFERENCE	↦ LENGTH
AT THE TRAILHEAD	**5.2 KM (LOOP)**
🔍 HIGHLIGHTS	〰 ELEVATION GAIN
PRISTINE MOUNTAIN LAKES	**128 METERS**

6060 STOUT

4.1 % ALCOHOL CONTENT

 CHOCOLATE BROWN

 SLIGHTLY SWEET MOCHA

 RICH CHOCOLATE

BITTERNESS

SWEETNESS

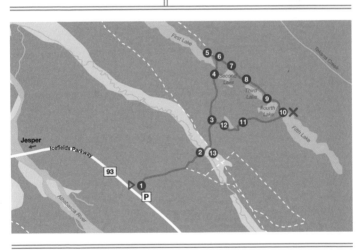

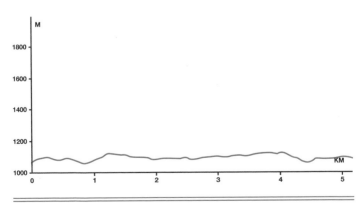

HIKE DESCRIPTION

Take a sweet hike in Canada's largest national park and be rewarded with alluring lake views five times over. Afterward, toast the beautiful mosaic of the Rockies with a dark stout at Jasper Brewing Company.

One of the best road trips in the world, the Icefields Parkway between Jasper and Banff will tempt you to stop in innumerable spots (starting with the daunting Columbia Icefields). But just ten minutes before you pull into the community of Jasper, this epic journey between national parks is punctuated by a five-star (or should I say "five-lake") hike that will introduce you to Canada's largest national park (spanning over 11,000 square kilometers) in a dazzling way. Jasper was named after Jasper Hawes, who managed a regional fur-trading post for the North West Company in the early 1800s. Hawes was a métis (a person of mixed European and Indigenous ancestry) who was originally from Maryland and was uprooted to Canada during the American Revolution. The site of the trading post is about a half-hour drive north of the town of Jasper.

Valley of the Five Lakes isn't a particularly challenging hike, but there are some steep sections that will make you feel like you've put in an effort. Taking the loop counterclockwise, you'll come upon the first lake soon after crossing the Wabasso Creek Bridge. But you won't have seen anything yet—the third and fourth lakes are considered the most beautiful. Parks Canada has placed over 200 red Adirondack chairs in peaceful, breathtaking locations all over Canada, and two of them are perched between lakes number three and four on this trail. If you've packed a lunch or a snack, this would be the place to loosen your laces and pause for a beat to appreciate the natural world around you. No one would mind, either, if you decided to wade in for a little swim in any one of these incredibly accessible mountain lakes that each glimmer with their own unique shade of blue or green. Reflect on what a treat your afternoon has been as you cap it off with 6060 chocolatey stout at Jasper Brewing Company, which is just down the road.

TURN-BY-TURN DIRECTIONS

1. From the parking lot, follow the wide path to the left of the toilets that leads into the forest.
2. At 0.8 km, turn left and cross the bridge.
3. At 0.9 km, take a right on Trail 9b and head uphill to begin the loop in a counterclockwise direction.
4. At 1.2 km, continue left to the first lake.
5. At 1.8 km, arrive at the first lake.
6. At 2.0 km, go right at the junction and continue on Trail 9a.
7. At 2.2 km, reach the second lake.
8. At 2.4 km, reach the third lake.

9. At 2.7 km, reach the fourth lake; the red chairs are on the right. From there, look for Trail 9a, which is marked by a yellow square on a tree to the left; continue on Trail 9a.
10. At 3.0 km, the fifth lake is on the left and the trail continues to the right. Head downhill to where "9a" is marked on a tree and cross a bridge.
11. At 3.6 km, at the top of the hill, go left, staying on Trail 9a.
12. At 4.0 km, finish the loop at a junction and turn right. A sign points back to the trailhead.
13. At 4.3 km, turn right and cross the bridge. Continue back to the lot on Trail 9a.

FIND THE TRAILHEAD

From Jasper, take Highway 93 south for just under 9 kilometers where there is a sign for Valley of the Five Lakes on the left. The trailhead parking lot is on the left.

JASPER BREWING COMPANY

The Jasper Brewing Company is a sister of the Banff Brewing Company, Last Best Brewing and Distilling in Calgary, and the Campio Brewing Company in Edmonton. All fall under the umbrella of Bearhill Brewing. Together, they make up what's been coined the "Albeerta" brand. All establishments were founded by three best friends: Brett Ireland, Alexander Derksen, and Socrates Korogonas, who were born and raised in Jasper. Jasper's 6060 Stout is a well-known local favorite. Head brewer Spike Baker says locals have been known to riot when it's not on tap, and that it's his favorite beer to brew. So, now that you're in the know, give it a go!

LAND MANAGER

Jasper National Park
500 Connaught Drive
Jasper, AB
T0E 1E0
(780) 852-6176
www.pc.gc.ca/en/pn-np/ab/jasper

BREWERY

Jasper Brewing Company
624 Connaught Drive
Jasper, AB
T0E 1E0
(780) 852-4111
www.jasperbrewingco.ca
Distance from trailhead: 10 kilometers

BEAVER BOARDWALK

THE WORLD'S LONGEST FRESHWATER BOARDWALK

HINTON
AB

▷··· STARTING POINT	···✗ DESTINATION
WEST END, MAXWELL LAKE	**OBSERVATION POINT, MAXWELL LAKE**
🍺 BREWERY	🎋 HIKE TYPE
FOLDING MOUNTAIN BREWING	**EASY** 🚶
🐾 DOG FRIENDLY	📅 SEASON
YES (LEASH REQUIRED)	**YEAR-ROUND**
$ FEES	🕐 DURATION
NONE	**1 HOUR 15 MIN.**
⛰ MAP REFERENCE	↦ LENGTH
AT TRAILHEAD	**3 KM (LOOP)**
🔍 HIGHLIGHTS	〰 ELEVATION GAIN
WORLD'S LONGEST FRESHWATER BOARDWALK, ACTIVE BEAVER DAM	**17 METERS**

FOLDING MOUNTAIN BREWING

ALPINE CRAN BERRY SOUR

Alberta Brewed

4.5% alc./vol.
Ale

4.5 %
ALCOHOL
CONTENT

**ALPINE
CRANBERRY SOUR**

MAGENTA

CRANBERRY,
HONEY,
CRACKERS

CRANBERRY,
HONEY

BITTERNESS

SWEETNESS

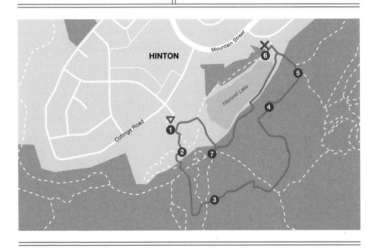

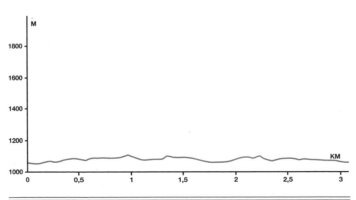

HIKE DESCRIPTION

Stroll along an enchanting boardwalk to an active beaver dam; then head into a forest teeming with wildlife and emerge on the shores of a stunning lake. Afterward, visit Folding Mountain and sample a one-of-a-kind cranberry sour.

For over 300 years, the beaver has been considered Canada's national icon. Before the fur trade began in the early 16th century, there were approximately six million beavers in what is now Canada, but by the mid-19th century, the population had been decimated. Due to conservation efforts and improved protection of floodplain habitats, beavers have made a comeback over the course of the last century. These stocky, buck-toothed creatures with their paddle-like tails can be found in rivers, creeks, and lakes all over Canada, and you can count on seeing them in the colony at Maxwell Lake.

The Maxwell Lake wetlands feature the world's longest freshwater boardwalk, which comprises more than three kilometers of walkway and interpretive signs. This may not be a lengthy hike, but you'll want to take your time meandering through the marshland and getting close to an active beaver dam and lodge. To make sure you see the beavers, visit during the warmer months. And beavers are more active in the early morning and in the evening, so you may want to plan your hike accordingly.

The area is also home to several species of ducks, muskrats, wood frogs, and bats. A segment of the boardwalk takes you through a forest corridor that is typical of many forested paths in the Rockies.

TURN-BY-TURN DIRECTIONS

1. From the trailhead, go right and cross a gravel path before stepping onto the boardwalk. Continue straight instead of turning left as you start off on the boardwalk. The beaver pond is straight ahead.
2. At 0.1 km, reach the beaver lodge. There are smaller dams along the way before you arrive at the lodge.
3. At 0.5 km, go right at the fork.
4. At 1.3 km, go right at the intersection. Then, after about 10 meters, turn right at a second intersection.
5. At 1.5 km, step off the boardwalk onto a dirt path in the forest; almost immediately, turn left and get back on the boardwalk.
6. At 1.8 km, arrive at Maxwell Lake and proceed to the observation point (a covered wooden platform). After leaving the observation point, continue along the boardwalk.
7. At 2.3 km, you'll arrive at another viewpoint for the beaver lodge. Continue along the east side of Maxwell Lake until you arrive back at the trailhead.

FIND THE TRAILHEAD

The Beaver Boardwalk is located south of the junction of Highway 16 and Mountain Street in Hinton. From the junction, follow Mountain Street South for 1.3 kilometers and then turn right at the second junction onto Collinge Road. Drive 150 meters and park in the town of Hinton parking lot. From the parking lot, walk 150 meters west along Collinge Road and turn left at the Maxwell Lake Apartments. The Beaver Boardwalk trailhead is behind the apartments at the west end of Maxwell Lake.

FOLDING MOUNTAIN BREWING

Folding Mountain Brewing stands at the base of Folding Mountain on the edge of Jasper National Park, minutes from Hinton, Alberta. The owners, Aric Johnson and Jason Griffiths, are Hinton locals and childhood friends who dabbled in home brewing before opening their brewery, taproom, and restaurant in 2017. Their recipe for success is simple—great beer with a great backdrop. Cranberries grow in many parts of Canada on low-lying vines in beds created by alpine glacial deposits. If you like a juicy tartness, these berries will bring a new Canadian flair to your repertoire of favorite beers. Pucker up!

LAND MANAGER

The Town of Hinton
131 Civic Centre Road
2nd Floor
Hinton, AB
T7V 2E5
(780) 865-6000
www.hinton.ca

BREWERY

Folding Mountain Brewing
49321 Folding Mountain Village
Yellowhead County, AB
T7V 1X3
(780) 817-6287
www.foldingmountain.com
Distance from trailhead: 22 kilometers

SWIFT CREEK LOOP

A GUSHING CREEK AND AN ENCHANTED FOREST

VALEMOUNT
BC

▷··· STARTING POINT	···✗ DESTINATION
YELLOWHEAD HIGHWAY	BRIDGE OVER SWIFT CREEK
🍺 BREWERY	▦ HIKE TYPE
THREE RANGES BREWING COMPANY	MODERATE
🐾 DOG FRIENDLY	📅 SEASON
YES (LEASH REQUIRED)	YEAR-ROUND
$ FEES	🕐 DURATION
NONE	2 HOURS 30 MIN.
⛰ MAP REFERENCE	↦ LENGTH
AT THE TRAILHEAD	9.3 KM (LOOP)
🔍 HIGHLIGHTS	〰 ELEVATION GAIN
SUSPENSION BRIDGE, OLD CEDARS, PICNIC TABLE WITH A VIEW	221 METERS

5.0 %
ALCOHOL CONTENT

**RAM'S HEAD
AMERICAN
AMBER ALE**

MEDIUM AMBER

BREADY,
CITRUSY,
CARAMEL

CARAMEL,
FRUITY,
HOPPY

BITTERNESS

SWEETNESS

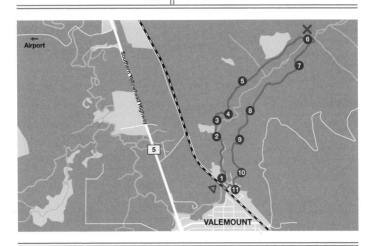

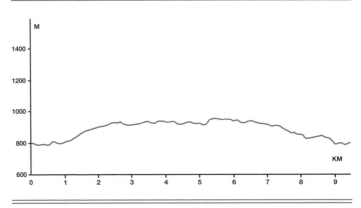

HIKE DESCRIPTION

A swiftly running creek, a stellar viewpoint, and the chance of spotting wild salmon will spur you on through an enchanting forest. Restore your strength post-hike with a Ram's Head Ale.

The town of Valemount is in the North Thompson Valley at the northern reach of the Rocky Mountain Trench in British Columbia. The Swift Creek hike begins where the first settlers lived during the building of the national railway. The settlement was called Swift Creek until it was relocated about one and a half kilometers down the track in 1927 and became known as Valley of the Mountains; this eventually morphed into Valemount. The land that would become Valemount was a traditional territory of First Nations peoples, including the Kootenai, Shuswap, and Rocky Mountain Cree. Today, it's a sought-after destination for both heli-hiking and heli-skiing in the nearby Cariboo Mountain range.

The first couple of kilometers of the hike are part of the out-and-back Swift Creek Viewpoint Trail, which soon passes by an exquisitely placed picnic table from which you can take in views of the village, Canoe Mountain, and the Premier Range, a group of mountains in the Cariboos. The Swift Creek Loop, popular with locals, continues for another 8.5 kilometers from here, leading you through a forest of lichens, mushrooms, and old cedars to a suspension bridge with the rush of Swift Creek sounding below. If hiking in the early fall, you might even see wild sockeye salmon spawning in the river! There's a good chance you'll be sharing this trail with bikers, so pay attention to the signs along the way differentiating the bike path from the hiking path to avoid any mishaps!

You may wish to pick up some homemade goodies at the Valemount Swiss Bakery as you head back into the village, to be washed down with a Ram's Head Amber Ale at Three Ranges Brewing Company.

TURN-BY-TURN DIRECTIONS

1. From the trailhead, follow the path down and into the woods. Swift Creek is on the right. Follow the wide gravel path up to the left.

2. At 1.0 km, come upon a sign on the right side of the path marking the 1.0 km point. Turn left and uphill on a narrower dirt path.

3. At 1.1 km, there's a sign for a bike trail. Don't follow the direction indicated by this sign; instead, take a sharp right and walk along the ridge above the creek.

4. At 1.8 km, reach the first viewpoint with a picnic table. There is a sign and a map on a tree to the left of the picnic table. Follow Trail #6.

5. At 2.7 km, reach a junction with a map and a sign. Take Trail #6 to the right and stay on it instead of taking the bike trail on the left.

6. At 4.5 km, reach the suspension bridge across Swift Creek. Cross the bridge. Trail #6 naturally turns right after the bridge.

7. At 5.3 km, cross a bike path and continue on Trail #6, which heads toward the right after the intersection and widens into a double-track path.

8. At 6.7 km, reach a sign on a tree reading Ale Trail Gravity Exit. Turn right on the Ale Trail.

9. At the fork at 7.4 km, continue to the left on the Ale Trail Gravity Exit. The trails heading right are the Southern Traverse and Tech Zone trails. Don't take these.

10. At 8.6 km, reach a road where the trail appears to end. The area straight ahead is private property. Look to the right and find the narrow path that continues into the bushes.

11. At 8.8 km, the path merges with Larch Street and continues into a residential area. Take Larch Street until it meets Juniper Street and then turn right on Juniper. Immediately come to a sign pointing back to the trailhead. Take the first left (Gordon Street) and head to Main Street. Turn right and walk back to the trailhead and parking area.

FIND THE TRAILHEAD

Head down 5th Avenue through downtown Valemount, cross the railway tracks, and then turn left onto Main Street and follow it for 1 kilometer. Parking is available on the west side of the road just before the bridge (across from the Golden Years Lodge). The trail starts immediately after the bridge on the right.

THREE RANGES BREWING COMPANY

The village of Valemount is situated between the Rocky, Monashee, and Cariboo Mountains. It's therefore fitting that this little resort town's only craft brewery is named "The Three Ranges." As its motto suggests, it's "putting the ale in Valemount." Husband-and-wife team Michael and Rundi Lewis have been working since 2013 to create beers reminiscent of everything that is distinctive about the Valemount region. The names of their beers reflect their love of the outdoors, with labels such as Ram's Head, Vail Trail XPA, Snow Dance Porter, Upswift Creek Pilsner (available October–March), and Alpenglow Amber Ale adorning their cans. Ram's Head is named for British Columbia's northern pioneers who, when they organized themselves for war in the late 19th century, chose a big-horned ram as their symbol. This amber ale is as rough and ready (and as strong) as those early Canadian pioneers.

LAND MANAGER

Valemount Trails Manager
785 Cranberry Lake Road
Valemount, BC
V0E 2Z0
(250) 566-9893
www.trails.visitvalemount.ca

BREWERY

Three Ranges Brewing Company
1160 5 Avenue
Valemount, BC
V0E 2Z0
(250) 566-0024
www.threeranges.com
Distance from trailhead: 1.4 kilometers

THE KOOTENAYS

JUNIPER TRAIL

JUNIPER BUSHES, A CANYON, AND A MAGICAL FOREST FULL OF BIGHORN SHEEP

RADIUM HOT SPRINGS, BC

▷··· STARTING POINT	···✖ DESTINATION
OVERFLOW PARKING LOT, RADIUM HOT SPRINGS	**SINCLAIR CANYON, SINCLAIR CREEK**
🍺 BREWERY	HIKE TYPE
RADIUM BREWING	**MODERATE**
🐾 DOG FRIENDLY	📅 SEASON
YES (LEASH REQUIRED)	**YEAR-ROUND**
$ FEES	⏱ DURATION
NATIONAL PARK ENTRANCE FEE	**2 HOURS 45 MIN.**
⛰ MAP REFERENCE	↦ LENGTH
AT TRAILHEAD	**5.7 KM (LOOP)**
🔍 HIGHLIGHTS	〰 ELEVATION GAIN
HOT SPRINGS, SPA, CANYON-FLOOR RIVER CROSSING	**297 METERS**

6.0 %
ALCOHOL CONTENT

REDSTREAK RED ALE

 RED

 CARAMEL, MAPLE SYRUP

 MAPLE SYRUP, MALT, CARAMEL

BITTERNESS	SWEETNESS

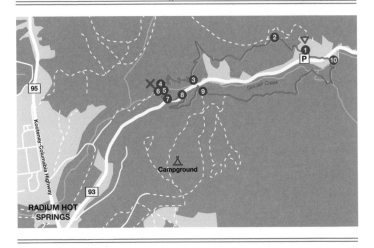

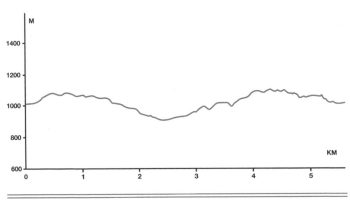

HIKE DESCRIPTION

Minutes from the highway, where you least expect it, is a treasure of a hike that leads to a canyon with waterfalls and a cliff walk through a forest full of bleating sheep. With an Irish ale waiting for you just down the road, this hike is spot on!

Radium Hot Springs in Kootenay National Park gets its name from the natural hot springs located five minutes east of town at the base of Red-streak Mountain. Here, surface water seeps through a deep fault, is heated in the depths of the earth, and returns to the surface in Sinclair Canyon. The pools, which are now a popular tourist attraction, were initially used by First Nations peoples; new infrastructure—a concrete bathing pool and bathhouse—was constructed by settlers when they arrived in the late 1800s. The location now includes a large hot pool, a cold plunge pool, a swimming pool, and a spa. The Juniper Trail begins at the Springs parking lot and delivers you right to the pools upon your return, so you can soak your tired muscles in healing, mineral-rich water post-hike. A small amount of radon (a weak radioactive substance produced by the decay of radium) has been found in the water at the site—enough to provide an intriguing name, but hardly enough to harm anyone.

This first part of the loop is a gradual climb; it's also where you should be on the lookout for juniper berries growing on the bushes if the season is right! While these small purple beads delightfully spice up a lamb dish and bring distinctive flavor to a gin martini, do keep in mind that it's illegal to pick anything in a national park. Just before descending into Sinclair Canyon (which was named after a 19th century–fur trading merchant), you'll come to a viewpoint with a bench and a lookout to the west. The highway is directly below you at this point, but the views of the Columbia Valley, the variety of the landscape, and the sound of waterfalls (and possibly the bleating of bighorn sheep) will have you tuning out the noise of the traffic.

On the floor of the canyon, with the light playing through the gorge and the water cascading down, you'll be able to take some beautiful photos. The wooden bridge that takes you across Sinclair Creek is the perfect spot to snap a few shots before climbing out of the canyon to take the return path on the other side of the highway. The trail on this side is steep in places but you'll have the aid of a series of switchbacks, and, eventually, stairs. Mind your step but do keep on the lookout for Rocky Mountain Bighorn Sheep! It's common to see these wild animals roaming here as they're attracted to the grassy mountain slopes. They aren't usually aggressive, but if it's rutting season (July–December) you may want to give them a wide berth if you encounter them on the trail.

Eventually, you'll wind your way down through a lush forest back toward the hot springs. Indulge in these medicinal waters before tipping back a craft beer at Radium Brewing. You'll cross the highway back to your car via an underground tunnel.

TURN-BY-TURN DIRECTIONS

1. From the parking lot, take the unmarked path leading up and away from the lot until you see a sign for the Juniper Trail.
2. At 0.4 km, reach the Juniper Trail and continue on it.
3. At 1.9 km, reach a viewpoint with a bench.
4. At 2.8 km, reach a bridge on the floor of the canyon and cross Sinclair Creek.
5. At 2.9 km, arrive at a lookout/rest point and take in a view of the falls.
6. At 3.0 km, turn left; continue on the Juniper Trail from the canyon floor instead of taking the trail straight ahead to the Redstreak Campground.
7. At 3.1 km, reach the highway. Turn left and walk up the sidewalk along the highway until you reach the falls viewpoint. Across the highway, you'll see a metal fence above the shoulder of the road where the path continues.
8. At 3.4 km, cross the highway to join the path on the other side (at the gate). There isn't an obvious crosswalk here, so be extra careful crossing the highway.
9. At 3,7 km, reach a set of stairs. At the top of the stairs, go left at the sign indicating toward Radium Hot Springs.
10. At 5.7 km, arrive at the Radium Hot Springs pools. Take the underpass and turn left to return to the parking lot.

FIND THE TRAILHEAD

From the roundabout in the village of Radium Hot Springs, take the Highway 93 exit east toward Banff National Park through Kootenay National Park. The hot springs are located 1.8 kilometers past the park gate. From the overflow parking lot for Radium Hot Springs (located on the left side of the highway as you approach the pools) look for the sign and trail map at the east end of the parking lot. To your left, you will see the trail leading up and into the trees, away from the lot.

RADIUM BREWING

Nestled against the headwaters of the Columbia River in Radium, British Columbia, this family-run nanobrewery finds inspiration in the gorgeous scenery around it to make fine traditional craft beers using an environmentally friendly process. The entire brewery was designed to be net zero, which means it produces as much energy as it uses over the course of a year. The brewers produce small batches so that they remain agile and are always creating different styles and recipes. Owners Stephen Gale and Jacob Houghton encourage beer lovers to share their ideas and recommend recipes. When these suggestions work out, money earned from customer-created beer gets donated to a local non-profit. Loosen your hiking boots in Radium's casual taproom or on their hospitable patio and enjoy an ale, lager, pilsner, or stout with a funky outdoorsy name. The brewery offers mead and wine as gluten-free options, and you're encouraged to grab a menu from any of the surrounding eateries and have a meal delivered to the brewpub if you're feeling peckish after your hike.

LAND MANAGER

Radium Hot Springs
7556 Main Street East
Radium Hot Springs, BC
VOA 1M0
(250) 347-9331
www.radiumhotsprings.com

BREWERY

Radium Brewing
7537 Mail Street W,
Radium Hot Springs, BC
VOA 1M0
(250) 688-8091
www.radiumbrewing.ca
Distance from trailhead: 3.2 kilometers

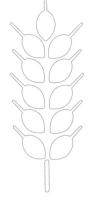

ELKHORN CABIN

PANORAMIC VISTAS AND A STUNNING RAVINE

PANORAMA
BC

▷⋯ STARTING POINT	⋯✗ DESTINATION
MILE 1 EXPRESS CHAIRLIFT	**ELKHORN CABIN**
🍺 BREWERY	HIKE TYPE
ARROWHEAD BREWING COMPANY	**STRENUOUS**
🐾 DOG FRIENDLY	📅 SEASON
NO	**LATE JUNE– EARLY SEPTEMBER**
$ FEES	⏱ DURATION
YES	**3 HOURS**
⛰ MAP REFERENCE	↦ LENGTH
PANORAMA MOUNTAIN RESORT	**6.6 KM (LOOP)**
🔍 HIGHLIGHTS	∿ ELEVATION GAIN
HIGH-SPEED CHAIRLIFT, PANORAMIC VIEWS	**731 METERS**

5.0 %
ALCOHOL
CONTENT

ORIGINAL '83
HONEY BROWN
ALE

 DARK AMBER

 BISCUITY

 LIGHT MALT,
HONEY

BITTERNESS	SWEETNESS

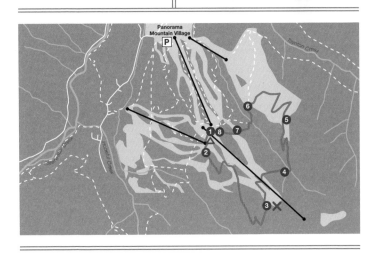

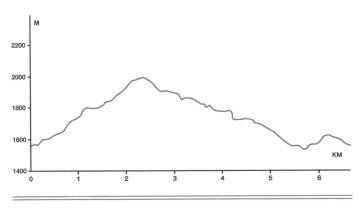

HIKE DESCRIPTION

Hike up to stunning views of the Kootenay Rockies before meandering down through a ravine and forest. Cap it off with a sweet-sippin' honey ale made with local bumblebee honey.

This hike at the Panorama Ski Resort starts out with an aerial view of the ski area from the Mile 1 Express ski lift. Jump on the high-speed chairlift to be transported up 380 meters for views of the Kootenay Rockies and Mount Nelson (the highest peak across the valley, with the flat top). Just off the chairlift at the top, you'll walk a few meters to the left to reach the trailhead. Founded in 1962 by Fritz Zehnder Guy Messerli of Switzerland, the resort has become a top international ski destination with 135 named trails and is known for its long cruising runs (the longest is 6.5 kilometers). In the summer months, apart from hiking trails, Panorama has one of the best downhill mountain bike parks in the Rockies. Expect to see a slew of helmeted riders with mountain bikes disembarking from the chairlift around you.

You'll begin the hike at an elevation of 1,560 meters, initially taking the Summit Trail, which is a ski hill access road. It's steep from the start and has no switchbacks, so poles are recommended! The trail does level out on occasion, providing your legs with welcome relief, but it's a tough slog right to the almost unnoticeable trail that leads you to the highpoint of the hike, the Elkhorn Cabin at 2,133 meters. The cabin sits midway down the Rollercoaster ski run and boasts some of the best views on the mountain. While closed during the summer months, it's an excellent spot to take a break before commencing the downhill walk back to the top of Mile 1 Express via the Cox Creek Trail and the Lynx Loop. It's possible you might see wildlife such as bears, deer, elk, moose, and coyotes on the slopes or around the village. Be sure to keep a keen eye out for grouse camouflaged amongst the bushes and rocks.

After the cabin, the trail is unmarked. You'll cross the Skyline ski run, heading toward a sign that reads "Founder's Ridge." Once on the trail, it's obvious where to go. You'll be on a wide access road that's easy to navigate. At the 8 kilometer mark, there will be a path leading off to your left which is not obvious; however, you'll see a white sign at the treeline reading "Cox Creek Trail," which becomes a narrow meandering path through trees and a ravine. There are regular signs on the trees marking the trail. After about half a kilometer you'll take a sharp left turn onto Lynx Loop, which brings you back to the path you originally set off on. Walk down to the loading zone for the chairlift and enjoy the ride as you descend to Panorama Village!

TURN-BY-TURN DIRECTIONS

1. From the trailhead, head up and to your right on the ski area access road.
2. At 0.4 km, follow the sign that reads "To Summit."
3. At 2.5 km, turn left on a narrow, unmarked trail and arrive at Elkhorn Cabin on the Skyline ski run. There is no visible path here, so look for a ski run sign across the slope that says "Founder's Ridge." Follow the direction indicated by the sign to stay on the trail.
4. At 3.1 km, keep left on the path as it is joined by another road from the right.
5. At 4.4 km, reach a viewpoint at a big rock.
6. At 5.7 km, reach a white sign posted on a tree off the main trail to the left on the Cox Creek Trail.
7. At 6.3 km, take a sharp left on the Lynx Loop (sign).
8. At 6.6 km, join the original trail and head back toward the chairlift.

FIND THE TRAILHEAD

From Invermere, drive 18 kilometers up Toby Creek Road to Panorama. From the Panorama ski area parking lot, walk toward the ski hill and take the Mile 1 Express high-speed chairlift to an elevation of 1,615 meters. Go left at the top of the lift. You will see the Panorama Bike Park down to your left; the trailhead for the Summit Trail will be above and to your right.

ARROWHEAD BREWING COMPANY

Situated in the popular summer town of Invermere in the Columbia Valley of British Columbia, the Arrowhead Brewery serves up six permanent beers as well as seasonal varieties. The owners, long-time Kootenay residents Shawn and Leanne Tegart, strive to bring a relaxed vibe to the craft beer experience with a 1950s-style taproom reminiscent of Gastown, Vancouver's first neighbourhood. The Tegarts once worked in woodworking and creative design; now they channel their creative energies into producing quality all-natural craft beer. The Original '83 brown ale is named for its 83 "Original Honeys": the women who answered the call to participate in its pin-up inspired photo shoot. (The result of the shoot can now be seen on a poster above the bar.) The beer is made with the brewery's own bumblebee honey! If you're checking out the seasonal brews, chances are you'll see some locally sourced berries on the lists of ingredients.

LAND MANAGER

Panorama Resort
2000 Panorama Drive
Panorama, BC
V0A 1T0
(800) 663-2929
www.panoramaresort.com

BREWERY/RESTAURANT

Arrowhead Brewing Company
481 Arrow Road
Invermere, BC
V0A 1K2
(778) 526-2739
www.arrowheadbrewingcompany.ca
Distance from trailhead: 23.3 kilometers (including chairlift ride)

BEGBIE FALLS

A SHADED WALK TO A WATERFALL AND BEACH

REVELSTOKE
BC

▷··· STARTING POINT	···✗ DESTINATION
BEGBIE CREEK	**UPPER ARROW LAKE**
🍺 BREWERY	🏁 HIKE TYPE
MT. BEGBIE BREWING CO.	**MODERATE**
🐾 DOG FRIENDLY	📅 SEASON
YES (LEASH REQUIRED)	**MAY–OCTOBER**
$ FEES	⏰ DURATION
NATIONAL PARK ENTRANCE FEE	**1 HOUR 45 MIN.**
🗻 MAP REFERENCE	↦ LENGTH
AT TRAILHEAD	**5.5 KM (ROUND-TRIP)**
🔍 HIGHLIGHTS	〰 ELEVATION GAIN
INLAND RAINFOREST, GLACIAL WATERFALL	**237 METERS**

HIGH COUNTRY KÖLSCH

 SLIGHTLY HAZY, STRAW

 WHITE GRAPE, GRASS, LEMON ZEST, BREADY

 BISCUIT, TART FRUIT, GRASSY

BITTERNESS   SWEETNESS

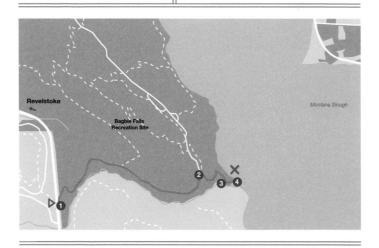

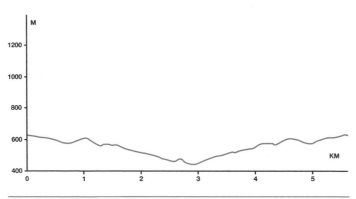

HIKE DESCRIPTION

A tranquil woodland hike along a creek brings you to a waterfall with a beach. With a crisp kölsch waiting to cut through your thirst, a day in the Rockies doesn't get any better!

Revelstoke, like so many other Canadian cities, has a history tied to the Canadian Pacific Railway. It's named after Lord Revelstoke, whose bank helped save the railway from bankruptcy in 1885.

The small city is situated within the world's only inland temperate rainforest (see Stoke Climb, Hike 19), which once spanned 40 million acres from Prince George in central British Columbia down through the Kootenays and south across the US border into Washington, Idaho, and Montana. Due to development and logging, only a portion of the rainforest still exists, making hikes in the old growth around Revelstoke a very special experience.

The hike to Begbie Falls is a relatively short one but it has major rewards. It begins in the rainforest on the lower part of Mount Macpherson. This little hike is a good bet even on a rainy day, thanks to the dense overstory of the rainforest that provides reliable cover. From the outset, you'll be walking along the trail that sport climbers use to access the crag above, and you'll see signs along the way pointing to various climbing walls. But don't worry, your route is an easy one: a well-marked, hard-packed dirt trail meandering downhill through a quiet mossy woodland. You'll be able to hear Begbie Creek rushing beside you most of the way, and in no time, you'll be standing on a viewing platform watching the cascade of glacial run-off from Mount Begbie. The mountain, with its triple peak, is an iconic symbol of Revelstoke and offers a challenging all-day summit hike for the more adventurous. You can choose to turn back after the falls, but it's only a short walk to Upper Arrow Lake, where you can sit for a while on a (rocky) beach, taking in the view of Revelstoke Mountain Resort across the valley.

TURN-BY-TURN DIRECTIONS

1. From the trailhead, follow the signed Mount Macpherson Bluff Trail into the woods.
2. At 2.1 km, hit an access road. Turn right onto the road and walk toward the parking lot, where a sign on the left points to the lower trailhead for Begbie Falls.
3. At 2.4 km, turn right at the sign pointing toward the falls. After 80 meters you'll arrive at the lookout platform for the falls. From here, return back to the sign for the falls and continue straight (instead of turning left to return to the trailhead).
4. At 2.8 km, you'll arrive at a day-use picnic site. Continue through the site, following the trail downward for a short distance to the beach at Upper Arrow Lake. Return the way you came.

FIND THE TRAILHEAD

To get to the Begbie Falls trailhead from Revelstoke, drive west on BC-1 and cross the Columbia River. Once you cross the bridge, turn left onto BC-23; after 9 kilometers, look for the first turnoff to the left, where there is a small parking lot and a kiosk.

MT. BEGBIE BREWING CO.

Mt. Begbie Brewing Co. is nestled on a hill above Revelstoke, away from the city's downtown core. It has a reputation for creating tried-and-true beer rather than so-called "trendy concoctions," but it does experiment with seasonal brews. Co-owner Bart Larson is originally from Revelstoke. He and his partner Tracey Larson were living in Van-couver when they opted for a lifestyle change and decided to move back to Bart's hometown. Bart's PhD in nuclear physics and Tracey's

Master's in zoology weren't exactly in high demand in the small city, so they put their scientific knowledge and creativity to good use and opened the brewery in 1996. In 2017, Mt. Begbie Brewery was named the Canadian Craft brewery of the year at the Canadian Brewing Awards. In the same year, its High Country Kölsch won best Kölsch-style ale at the World Beer Awards.

LAND MANAGER

Mount Revelstoke National Park
Meadows in the Sky Parkway
Revelstoke, BC
V0E 2S0
(250) 837-7500
www.pc.gc.ca/en/pn-np/bc/revelstoke

BREWERY

Mt. Begbie Brewing Co.
2155 Oak Drive
Revelstoke, BC
V0E 2S1
(250) 837-2756
www.mt-begbie.com
Distance from trailhead: 16.5 kilometers

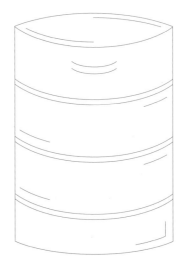

STOKE CLIMB

FROM TEMPERATE RAINFOREST TO ALPINE FLORA

REVELSTOKE MOUNTAIN RESORT, BC

▷⋯ STARTING POINT	⋯✕ DESTINATION
REVELATION GONDOLA UPPER STATION	**BENCH BELOW MOUNT MACKENZIE SUB-SUMMIT**
🍺 BREWERY	HIKE TYPE
RUMPUS BEER COMPANY	**MODERATE**
🐾 DOG FRIENDLY	SEASON
NOT PERMITTED ON GONDOLA	**SUMMER/FALL**
$ FEES	⏱ DURATION
GONDOLA, NATIONAL PARK ENTRANCE FEE	**4 HOURS**
⛰ MAP REFERENCE	↦ LENGTH
AT TRAILHEAD	**14 KM (ROUND-TRIP)**
👁 HIGHLIGHTS	〰 ELEVATION GAIN
SUBALPINE RAINFOREST, GONDOLA, ALPINE FLOWERS	**529 METERS**

6.0 %
ALCOHOL CONTENT

SPACE NUGS PALE ALE

 SLIGHTLY HAZY AMBER

 GRAPEFRUIT AND LIGHT SPICE

 CITRUSY HOPS AND SILKY OATS WITH CRISP DRY FINISH

BITTERNESS

SWEETNESS

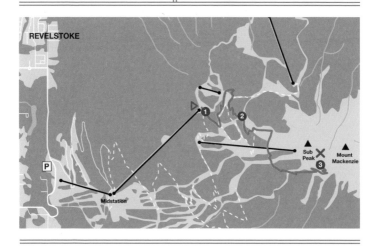

REVELSTOKE

Sub Peak   Mount Mackenzie

Midstation

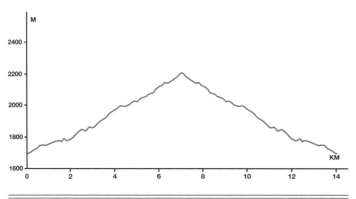

HIKE DESCRIPTION

Switchbacks through a subalpine rainforest make for a pleasurable climb up to alpine flora and stellar views. Back in the valley, replenish and chill with a pale ale in downtown "Revi."

Revelstoke Mountain Resort on Mount Mackenzie is known for record-breaking snowfalls and the steepest ski trails in North America. It's also in the middle of the world's only inland temperate rainforest. This interior wet belt is due to weather systems that come from the Pacific Ocean and rise over the Columbia Mountains. Like coastal rainforests, the moist-to-wet forests that result from this weather pattern are

predominantly old growth. The conditions develop inland because of high snow melt during the early part of the growing season and increased rainfall in the middle of the growing season.

You'll first take a twenty-minute gondola ride to midmountain, where the trail and the views begin. Alternatively, you can add an extra 3.8 kilometers to the hike by walking up a rather punishing slope called "Kill the Banker." From the top of the gondola, you'll see the rails of the Pipe Mountain Coaster, whose bright yellow carts descend the slopes and offer an alternative post-hike route (at additional cost) down the mountain. Once off the gondola, you'll immediately find yourself wandering through the rainforest at mid-elevation; here you'll be surrounded by old growth, such as Engelmann spruce and subalpine fir. The rainforest ends at tree line, and you'll begin to walk on alpine tundra, an important habitat for grizzly bears, mountain goats, and the endangered mountain caribou. You'll see many lichens up here, and, despite the short growing season at this elevation, numerous alpine flowers and grasses that thrive on the meadows during the summer months.

The route is also a single-track mountain-bike path and an access route for "Fifty-Six Twenty," a mountain-bike descent named for the resort's 5,620 feet of vertical lift-access terrain, so you'll be sharing the trail with bikers making their ascent. Approaching the sub-summit, you'll pass through alpine meadows bursting with wildflowers like lupines, fireweed paintbrush, and mountain arnica, and you'll experience incredible views of the Columbia River valley, with the Monashee mountains to the west and the Selkirks to the South. Experienced hikers have the option of continuing from the sub-summit on the 1.9-kilometer Subpeak Loop, a 45-minute trail that forms a circle just below the summit of Mount Mackenzie and offers 360-degree views of the surrounding mountains. The trail is straightforward and well-marked. Occasionally, you'll cross access roads, but there is excellent signage (yellow blazes and blue signs that read "Stoke Climb") indicating the way.

TURN-BY-TURN DIRECTIONS

1. From the trailhead, follow the signage for "Stoke Climb" into the rainforest.
2. At 2.6 km, emerge from the rainforest onto the alpine tundra and enjoy a nice view of the valley; continue on the Stoke Climb Trail.
3. At 7.0 km, reach a bench and see a pole with a blue blaze marking your destination. Return the way you came.

FIND THE TRAILHEAD

From downtown Revelstoke, travel west on Victoria Road. Take the second exit at the roundabout onto Fourth Street. Follow Fourth Street across the Illecillewaet Bridge and up a small hill; then turn left onto Nichol Road at the four-way intersection. Turn right onto Camozzi Road, which will lead you to the base of the resort. From the parking lot of the Sutton Place Hotel, walk past the hotel toward the ski hill. You'll see the gondola loading area at the base of the hotel.

From the top of Revelation Gondola, the trail begins just past the beacon search area, across from the start of the Guilt Trip Trail.

RUMPUS BEER COMPANY

Brewer and Rumpus co-owner Fred Orndorff was working at Eldo Brewery in Colorado when he met his future wife and co-owner, Dana Orndorff, who was on vacation from Canada. After a few years of a long-distance relationship, a road trip took them through Revelstoke, an event that would eventually lead them to their new home and a new vocation as brewery owners. The atmosphere at Rumpus is cozy and comfortable, like that of a rumpus room. The lineup, posted on a blackboard above the bar, is constantly changing, but the citrusy, crisp Space Nugs Pale Ale is almost always in the rotation. Rumpus is an on-premise, draught-only brewery with pints and flights of *beer* served exclusively in-house. That said, you can also purchase growlers and crowlers, fill them with what's on tap, and take them with you.

LAND MANAGER

Revelstoke Mountain Resort
2950 Camozzi Road
Revelstoke, BC
V0E 2S1
(866) 373-4753
www.revelstokemountainresort.com

BREWERY

Rumpus Beer Company
208 1 Street East B231
Revelstoke, BC
V0E 2S0
(250) 683-8100
www.rumpusbeerco.com
Distance from trailhead: 6 kilometers (plus a 3.4 kilometer gondola ride)

UPPER KASLO RIVER TRAIL

HIKE THE MOSSY KASLO RIVER VALLEY

KASLO
BC

▷··· STARTING POINT	···✕ DESTINATION
KASLO–NEW DENVER HIGHWAY	**VIEWPOINT KASLO WEST ROAD**
🍺 BREWERY	🔀 HIKE TYPE
ANGRY HEN BREWING CO.	**MODERATE** 🚶
🐾 DOG FRIENDLY	📅 SEASON
YES (LEASH REQUIRED)	**YEAR-ROUND**
$ FEES	🕐 DURATION
NONE	**1 HOUR 40 MIN.**
⛰ MAP REFERENCE	↦ LENGTH
AT TRAILHEAD	**7 KM (LOOP)**
🔍 HIGHLIGHTS	〰 ELEVATION GAIN
KOOTENAY LAKE, FOREST BOARDWALK, COVERED BRIDGES	**213 METERS**

HAPPY PILLS
EUROPEAN
PILSNER

4.8 %
ALCOHOL
CONTENT

 LIGHT GOLD

 FLORAL,
HERBAL,
HOP

 GRAIN,
FLORAL,
CRISP

BITTERNESS

SWEETNESS

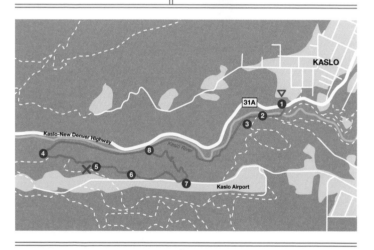

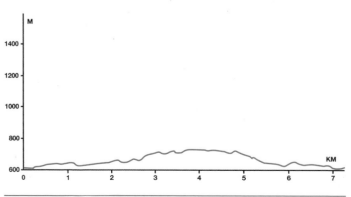

HIKE DESCRIPTION

This hike explores a mossy forest that features bridges and board-walks, with an airport runway thrown in to mix it up. After your adventure, return to the lakeside for special brews with creative names at the Angry Hen Brewery, owned and operated by women.

The picturesque town of Kaslo sits on the shores of Kootenay Lake, with the Purcell Mountains rising up above it. From the lake, the Kaslo river flows inland to a network of river trails dotted with charming bright red bridges. The upper trail begins just off the Kaslo–New Denver high-way. You'll be surprised by the beautiful, covered Trailblazers Bridge (just by the parking lot, but initially concealed). The moisture and spray from the river as you cross the bridge make for an inspired start to this trek, which winds through the narrow Kaslo River Valley.

As you step onto the Lettrari Loop soon after the bridge, you might spot some of the wildlife the area is known for, such as mule deer, lynx, northern alligator lizards, white tailed deer, moose, or bears. If you're a birdwatcher, keep on the lookout for bluebirds and great blue herons. The trail delivers a few surprises along the way. A beautiful, long board-walk curves back and forth through a mossy forest just before you emerge from the trees and onto a road next to the Kaslo airport runway! Here you can take in a spectacular view of Mount Kaslo across the valley.

Fun fact: Kaslo is also home to the world's oldest passenger stern-wheeler, the *SS Moyie*, which is an international treasure.

TURN-BY-TURN DIRECTIONS

1. From the parking spot off the highway, take the path down the steps to the Trailblazers Bridge. Cross the bridge.
2. At 0.2 km, go straight at the fork on the Lettrari Loop.
3. At 0.4 km, go right on the Lettrari Loop, which you'll walk counterclockwise.
4. At 2.6 km, reach the far end of Lettrari Loop. Here the path begins to climb.
5. At 3.7 km, reach Kaslo West Road and the viewpoint next to the Kaslo Airport runway. Walk along the road for about 50 meters and then follow the direction indicated by the Lettrari Loop trail sign on your left.
6. At 3.9 km, pass a bench with a view of Mount Kaslo and the Kaslo Valley. Continue on the Lettrari Loop.
7. At 4.4 km, go left on the Paul's Balls Trail and head back toward the river.
8. At 5.2 km, reach the Lettrari Loop path next to the river and return to the bridge.

FIND THE TRAILHEAD

About a half mile before arriving in Kaslo from the west, you'll encounter a "Welcome to Kaslo" sign. Pull into the large pullout there and you'll see a sign and map for the Kaslo River Trail. Alternatively, from Kaslo, take Avenue A, turn left onto Highway 31, and follow it for about a kilometer. The pullout parking area will be on your right.

ANGRY HEN BREWERY

This brewery is proud to have an almost all-woman team brewing tasty beer with intriguing names, pouring pints, and working behind the scenes to make this little gem of a brewery the creative place it is. Angry Hen was founded by Shirley Warne in 2017. Warne started home brewing as a hobby decades ago; she became known in the world of beer through her successful consultancy services offered to breweries across Canada before deciding to open her own brewery in Kaslo. Angry Hen's Happy Pills is a light and crisp traditional European Pilsner that'll go down smoothly after an afternoon hitting the trails. Examples of some other fun beer names at the Angry Hen include a classic Dusseldorf style Altbier called CTRL+ALT+DELETE; a lager called Fugue State; and a double IPA called Capon Rockin' in the Free World. The Kluckin' Kölsch sounds mighty tempting too! Located close to the shores of Kootenay Lake, Angry Hen offers a cozy nest after outdoor explorations, complete with a patio and stellar views of the Purcell Range and Selkirk Mountain.

LAND MANAGER

Kaslo Outdoor Recreation and Trails Society
Box 1024
Kaslo, BC
V0G 1M0
(250) 551-3028
www.kortsbc.blogspot.com

BREWERY

Angry Hen Brewery
343 Front Street
Kaslo, BC
V0G 1M0
(250) 353-7446
www.angryhenbrewing.com
Distance from the trailhead: 1.9 kilometers

PULPIT ROCK

A FAVORITE MORNING WORKOUT FOR NELSON LOCALS

NELSON
BC

▷⋯ STARTING POINT	⋯✕ DESTINATION
JOHNSTONE ROAD, NELSON	PULPIT ROCK
🍺 BREWERY	🀫 HIKE TYPE
NELSON BREWING COMPANY	MODERATE 🚶
🐾 DOG FRIENDLY	📅 SEASON
YES	EARLY APRIL– EARLY NOVEMBER
$ FEES	🕐 DURATION
NONE	1 HOUR 45 MIN.
⛰ MAP REFERENCE	↦ LENGTH
AT THE TRAILHEAD	4.1 KM (ROUND-TRIP)
🔍 HIGHLIGHTS	〰 ELEVATION GAIN
PANORAMIC VIEWS OF NELSON, RIDGE LOOKOUT BENCH	327 METERS

HOOLIGAN PILSNER

5.0 % ALCOHOL CONTENT

 MEDIUM GOLD

 BISCUITY, EARTHY, WHITE PEPPER

 CRACKERY, GRITTY, TOUCH OF CARAMEL

BITTERNESS

SWEETNESS

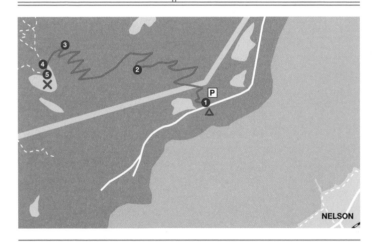

NELSON

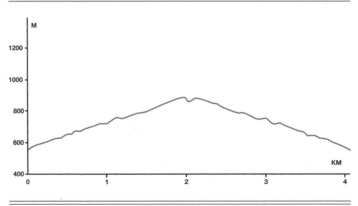

HIKE DESCRIPTION

Make this energetic ascent to panoramic views over the city of Nelson before pitching back a pilsner in a brewery that dates back over 125 years.

Pulpit Rock has been dubbed the local "walk in the park." That said, keep in mind that Nelson folk are a rather fit bunch! It's alleged that Pulpit Rock has had Nelsonites hiking it for nearly a century as there used to be mining sites on the mountain. Nelson is situated in the Selkirk Mountains and sits on the shores of Kootenay Lake's west arm. Picturesque, charming, hippie, and cosmopolitan are all words that have been used to describe this little city that's been featured in several Hollywood films—*Roxanne*, *The Age of Adaline*, and *Snow Falling on Cedars*, to name a few.

The Pulpit Rock hike runs up the spine of a mountain that locals refer to as Elephant Mountain. The well-worn trail is clearly marked and meanders through a series of short switchbacks that efficiently elevate you over 300 meters to an unobstructed view of the city and surrounding mountain ranges. If you don't have your own hiking poles and feel you might need some extra support, there's often a stash of them at the trailhead—yours to borrow on the honor system. As you arrive at Pulpit Rock, you'll see a sign to your right pointing upward to an extension known as Flagpole. This will add another 2.2 kilometers to your round-trip journey should you decide to take things a little further.

If you've had enough climbing for the day, there's a bench on the ridge where you can take a break and perhaps start thinking about your final destination by trying to spot the Nelson Brewing Company on the sloped streets of the city below. With a cool crisp Hooligan Pilsner on your mind, you may want to pay extra attention on that downhill descent.

TURN-BY-TURN DIRECTIONS

1. From the parking lot take the cement stairs up into the woods.
2. At 0.8 km, there's a sign pointing in the direction of the main trail. Go right onto this.
3. At 1.9 km, go right on an easier route or left on a more difficult route. The more difficult one is not too challenging, just a bit rockier.
4. At 2.0 km, reach a fork. Go left to make your way to Pulpit rock.
5. At 2.1 km, reach a bench at Pulpit Rock. Return the way you came.

FIND THE TRAILHEAD

To get to the parking area for Pulpit Rock from Nelson, head north on BC-3A for 1.8 kilometers and then turn left on Johnstone Road. Continue for 2.2 kilometers to reach the trailhead parking lot on the right.

NELSON BREWING COMPANY

In 1892, the original Nelson Brewing and Ice Company was founded in the same 125-year-old building on Latimer Street that today houses the Nelson Brewing Company. The building was left unoccupied for 40 years after 1956, when the brewery moved a little way down the road to Creston. Eventually, in 1991, a group of local businessmen reopened the Nelson Brewing Company in its original building. By 2006, it had become BC's largest fully certified organic brewery. It has a range of core beers that includes a pair of Hooligans (a Pale Ale and a Pilsner that placed first in the North American Light Beer category at the 2018 BC Beer Awards), the Harvest Moon Kölsch Hemp Ale, the Wild Honey Ale, the Bent Pole Northwest IPA, and the Valhalla Hazy Pale Ale. It also features seasonal beers and a wide range of highly creative small batch–limited release beers. Written on the can of The Hooligan Pilsner is the following: "A classic Pilsner that's bold and built for adventure." After a summer of hiking, this author highly agrees!

LAND MANAGER

Friends of Pulpit Rock
www.pulpitrock.ca

BREWERY

Nelson Brewing Company
512 Latimer Street
Nelson, BC
V1L 4T9
(250) 352-358
Distance from trailhead: 6.2 kilometers

MEL DE ANNA TRAIL LOOP

FOREST FLOOR HIKE AROUND A TRANQUIL POND

CASTELGAR
BC

▷⋯ STARTING POINT	⋯✕ DESTINATION
HIGHWAY 3	**FAR END OF CHAMPION PONDS**
🍺 BREWERY	🀫 HIKE TYPE
TAILOUT BREWING	**EASY**
🐾 DOG FRIENDLY	📅 SEASON
YES	**YEAR-ROUND**
$ FEES	🕐 DURATION
NONE	**2 HOURS**
⛰ MAP REFERENCE	↦ LENGTH
AT THE TRAILHEAD	**5.5 KM (LOLLIPOP LOOP)**
👁 HIGHLIGHTS	∿ ELEVATION GAIN
WOODLAND PONDS, VIEWS OF THE COLUMBIA RIVER	**136 METERS**

SINGLE SPEY IPA

CLEAR GOLD

CITRUS,
PINE

CITRUSY,
PINEY

BITTERNESS   SWEETNESS

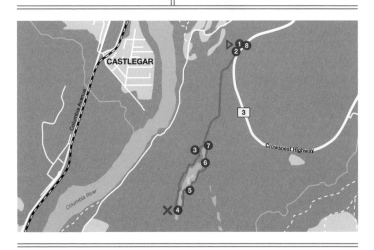

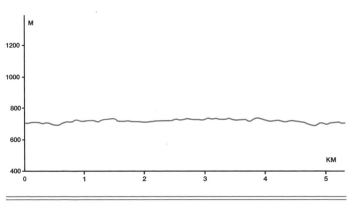

HIKE DESCRIPTION

Follow a forested loop through a pond ecosystem and delight in the remnants of the region's fur-trading and mining past. After your hike, hop down to Tailout Brewing for a delectable IPA.

What the Mel de Anna Trail lacks in elevation gain, it delivers in compelling terrain. You'll set off on a forest trail that gently ascends and descends and eventually rounds a marshy woodland area called Champion Ponds. Along the way, you'll experience superb views of the town of Castlegar and the Columbia River below. This is an interpretive trail with 16 stations that provide information about the area's flora and fauna. Pro tip: If you can plan this hike in the fall, you'll be treated to a symphony of golden larches and poplar trees.

Whatever the season, you'll pass under dwarf mistletoe clinging to hemlock trees, ponderosa pines, and other conifers as you navigate around numerous boulder-sized glacial erratics (rocks that were transported by a glacier long ago and deposited when the ice receded). Once you've passed the ponds, you'll encounter traces of the past: the ruins of an old cabin that might have belonged to a fur trapper or a miner, and the entrance to a mining shaft dug in the early 1900s by prospectors fruitlessly looking for gold. This deep, dark cave just off the trail extends about 15 meters into the bedrock. The Mel deAnna Trail is also known as an excellent place to birdwatch. Look up and you might see a red-tail hawk homing in on pond-dwelling prey such as frogs and snakes!

This enjoyable, accessible hike is located just minutes from the small city of Castlegar in the Selkirk Mountains, at the confluence of the Kootenay and Columbia Rivers. Castlegar is a sportsperson's playground, particularly well-known as a fishing destination. If you know a thing or two about the sport, you'll want to swap stories over an IPA with the owner of Tailout Brewing—that is, once you've worked up a good thirst on this fun and educational jaunt through the woods!

TURN-BY-TURN DIRECTIONS

1. From the parking lot, follow the Mel DeAnna Trail up past the bathrooms and scenic benches and through a gate in the chain-link fence.

2. At 0.1 km, there's a viewpoint with a bench.

3. At 1.6 km, at the junction, go left to set off counterclockwise on the loop.

4. At 2.6 km, cross the stream at the far end of the ponds and continue back on the other side of the ponds.

5. At 3.1 km, pass in front of the mining shaft.

6. At 3.5 km, there's a viewpoint and a bench at the end of a short spur that heads off the trail.

7. At 3.9 km, end the loop and turn right onto the trail going back to the parking lot.

8. At 5.5 km, arrive back at the trailhead.

FIND THE TRAILHEAD

Leaving Castlegar, drive a few minutes up Highway 3 toward Salmo. As the highway ascends, watch for a rest area with a sign reading "Mel DeAnna Trail" on the right.

TAILOUT BREWING

If you're familiar with sportfishing—one of fisheries biologist Hedin Nelson-Chorney's favorite pastimes—you'll immediately appreciate the name he chose for his brewery when he opened it in late 2019. "Tailout" refers to the shallow parts of a river where fish tend to gather. If you're just a lover of craft beer angling for a good recommendation, you can't go wrong with Tailout's Single Spey IPA, which is named for the two-handed fly rod ("spey rod"). Just like the rod, this IPA is perfectly balanced. One sip and you're sure to be hooked. You're welcome to bring your own food and listen to the live music at Castlegar's only craft brewery; during the summer months, however, Canada's own poutine will be on the menu to satisfy your hunger after an afternoon on the trail. Patrons of Tailout will be afforded the latest fishing and snow reports, with no shortage of epic pictures. You're urged to join them in the taproom with your own stories of adventure.

LAND MANAGER

Regional District of Central Kootenay
Nelson Office
202 Lakeside Drive
Nelson, BC
V1L 5R4
(250) 352-6665
www.rdck.ca

BREWERY

Tailout Brewing
1810 8th Avenue
Unit A
Castlegar, BC
V1N 2Y2
(250) 608-9056
www.tailoutbrewing.com
Distance from trailhead: 7.6 kilometers

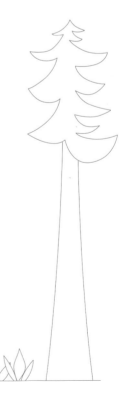

HUNDRED-ACRE WOOD OLD-GROWTH FOREST

AN OLD-GROWTH GROVE OF CEDARS AND HEMLOCKS

ROSSLAND BC

▷⋯ STARTING POINT	⋯✕ DESTINATION
HIGHWAY 3B	**BEAR BENCH**
🍺 BREWERY	HIKE TYPE
ROSSLAND BEER COMPANY	**EASY**
🐾 DOG FRIENDLY	SEASON
YES (LEASH REQUIRED)	**YEAR-ROUND**
$ FEES	🕐 DURATION
NONE	**45 MIN.**
🗺 MAP REFERENCE	↦ LENGTH
AT TRAILHEAD	**3 KM (LOLLIPOP LOOP)**
🔍 HIGHLIGHTS	〰 ELEVATION GAIN
INLAND RAINFOREST, HAND-CARVED WOODEN BENCH	**84 METERS**

ROSSLAND
GENUINE DRAFT
AMERICAN LAGER

5.0% ALCOHOL CONTENT

PALE YELLOW

BUBBLEGUM,
SULPHUR,
PINEY

LIGHT,
FULL-BODIED,
SWEET

BITTERNESS

SWEETNESS

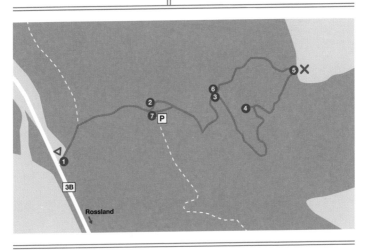

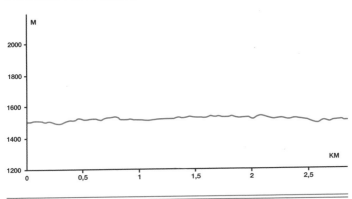

HIKE DESCRIPTION

Enjoy an immersive educational experience in a precious old-growth forest followed by a light lager chaser.

The old-growth forest outside of Rossland in the West Kootenays is part of British Columbia's inland temperate rainforest. These "at-risk" old-growth stands store large amounts of carbon, which helps mitigate climate change, and are home to wolverines, mountain caribou, western screech owls, and pileated woodpeckers. The trail through the 100-Acre Wood has interpretive signs along the way that delve into forest diversity, the climate, wildlife, and local history. It includes a stop in a wallow—a wetland gathering place for local fauna to "wallow," or roll about in the mud. This is an ideal spot to pause and search for footprints, or even try to spot some of the creatures that live in the forest around you. Although this is not a long hike, it's an opportunity to slow down and contemplate both the wonder and fragility of the inland rainforest. Halfway along the loop, at the forest's edge, a beautiful wooden bench with hand-carved bears provides another opportunity to absorb the medley of nature in this unique region of the Canadian Rockies.

TURN-BY-TURN DIRECTIONS

1. From the parking lot, head down the only gravel road for 100 meters, where there is a wooden sign on a tree at a junction reading "100-Acre Wood," with an arrow pointing toward the forest.
2. At 0.4 km, arrive at a second parking lot. On the left is another sign welcoming visitors to the 100-Acre Wood. There is also a map. Follow the indicated trail.
3. At 0.7 km, start off on the loop trail by going right.
4. At 1.3 km, detour left at the sign pointing toward the "Wallow"; then retrace your steps back to the main path.
5. At 1.6 km, reach the wooden bear bench at the edge of the forest.
6. At 2.0 km, arrive at the end of the loop trail and go right.
7. At 2.4 km, arrive back at the second parking lot. Head right to return to the trailhead.

FIND THE TRAILHEAD

From downtown Rossland, drive 15.5 kilometers north on Highway 3B and look for the sign on the right side of the highway for the 100-Acre Wood Old Growth Forest Walk.

ROSSLAND BEER COMPANY

Rossland Beer Company serves up award-winning beer in this historic mining community. It's owned and operated by best friends Petri Raito and Ryan Arnaud, who first delved into the world of beer-making when they opened Trail Brewing, a micro-brewery with a u-brew format (selling

ingredients and services for customers to make their own beer for private consumption). Now at a new location in central Rossland, they view their tasting room and patio as a gathering place for friends, family, and the streams of tourists they welcome each year. Several varieties of beer are always (and solely) on tap, including the refreshing, highly carbonated American Lager. Crowlers and growlers are also available. Rossland is perched on a hill in the beautiful Kootenays, and you'd genuinely be hard pressed to find a more glorious location to appreciate a good beer.

LAND MANAGER

The Kootenay Columbia Trail Society
information@kcts.ca
www.kcts.ca

BREWERY

Rossland Beer Company
1990F Columbia Avenue
Rossland, BC
V0G 1Y0
(250) 362-2122
www.rosslandbeer.com
Distance from trailhead: 15 kilometers

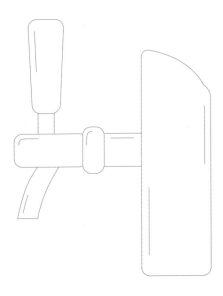

MIRAL HEIGHTS AND BLUFFS TRAIL

A FOREST ASCENT TO VIEWS OF COLUMBIA VALLEY

TRAIL
BC

▷··· STARTING POINT	···✕ DESTINATION
ALBERT DRIVE	**THE BLUFF**
🍺 BREWERY	HIKE TYPE
TRAIL BEER REFINERY	**MODERATE**
🐾 DOG FRIENDLY	SEASON
YES (LEASH REQUIRED)	**EARLY APRIL– EARLY NOVEMBER**
$ FEES	⏱ DURATION
NONE	**1 HOUR 45 MIN.**
⛰ MAP REFERENCE	↦ LENGTH
AT TRAILHEAD	**6.2 KM (LOLLIPOP LOOP)**
🔍 HIGHLIGHTS	〰 ELEVATION GAIN
VIEWS OF THE SEVEN SUMMITS RANGE, THE DEWDNEY TRAIL	**204 METERS**

**TRAIL ALE
AMERICAN RED**

 AMBER

 FRESH,
CRISP

 CARAMEL,
LIGHT FRUIT,
SLIGHTLY CITRUS

BITTERNESS   SWEETNESS

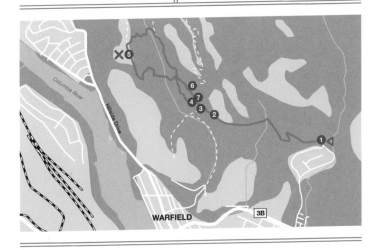

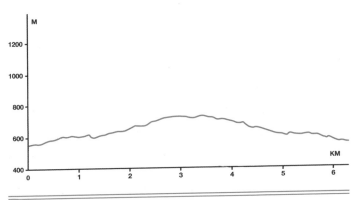

HIKE DESCRIPTION

A gradual incline on a delightful pathway to jaw-dropping views of the Columbia River. And what better way to finish your excursion than with a trail ale in a little city named Trail? Happy trails!

In the mid-19th century, a 720-kilometer trade route that cut through forests, rose over mountains, and navigated valleys was built to connect Hope, BC to Fort Steele in the interior of the province. The Dewdney Trail, as it was called, was a major transportation route for trappers, miners, and new settlers. Long before Europeans arrived, however, the land was home to the Salish people, who moved throughout the area looking for game and harvesting the many berries that grew there. The town of Trail, which is located on the Columbia River between the Monashee Mountains to the west and the Selkirk mountains to the east, gets its name from the long and well-worn Dewdney Trail. From a starting point very close to town, an enjoyable switch-backing route through a forest leads you to an impressive viewpoint over the Columbia River Valley. You'll know you're on the bluff when you spot a Canadian flag blowing in the wind. If the weather permits, you'll be able to see the peaks of the Seven Summits Range to the west.

TURN-BY-TURN DIRECTIONS

1. From the parking lot, head east up the hill and into the woods on the Miral Heights Trail.
2. At the fork at 1.5 km, continue straight.
3. At 1.6 km, go right onto the Bluffs Trail. The path to the left is a continuation of the Miral Heights Trail.
4. At 1.7 km, go left at the fork.
5. At 3.1 km, reach the Canadian flag at the top of the bluff: your destination. From here, turn right, following signage for the Bluff's Trail.
6. At 4.4 km, bear right on the Bluff's Trail.
7. At 4.6 km, the Bluffs Trail loop ends. Return the way you came on the Miral Heights Trail to the parking lot.

FIND THE TRAILHEAD

From the city of Trail, head northeast on Victoria Street/BC-3BE for 2.1 kilometers. Turn left onto McBride Street and continue for 1.1 kilometers. Turn left onto Albert Drive and continue straight to arrive at the parking lot and trailhead.

TRAIL BEER REFINERY

From outside the brewery on Bay Avenue in Trail, you'll see a factory high atop the hill with plumes of smoke rising from the stacks. This is the world's largest zinc and lead smelting and refining complex. When local business partners joined together in 2017 to open the Trail Beer Refinery, the city's first craft brewery, they chose a name tied to the area's main industry. The influence of the factory on the hill is also realized in the establishment's décor and the branding of both the brewery and full-service restaurant. If you like local trivia and are looking for a way to get to know the locals while imbibing your caramelly Trail Ale, ask where the name of the local hockey team, the Smoke Eaters, comes from. The conversation should flow as smoothly as the smoke rising from the hilltop after that.

LAND MANAGER

Kootenay Columbia Trail Society
information@kcts.ca
www.kcts.ca

BREWERY

Trail Beer Refinery
1299 Bay Avenue
Trail, BC
V1R 4A5
(778) 456-2827
Distance from trailhead: 2 kilometers

DELAURENTIIS BLUFFS LOOKOUT

AN EXCITING ASCENT TO SENSATIONAL VIEWS

SALMO
BC

▷··· STARTING POINT	···✗ DESTINATION
DELAURENTIIS ROAD	**VIEWPOINT ABOVE SALMO**
🍺 BREWERY	HIKE TYPE
EERIE CREEK BREWING COMPANY	**STRENUOUS**
🐾 DOG FRIENDLY	SEASON
YES (LEASH REQUIRED)	**YEAR-ROUND (APRIL—OCTOBER RECOMMENDED)**
$ FEES	⊘ DURATION
$10/DAY PASS	**2 HOURS 30 MIN.**
⚠ MAP REFERENCE	↦ LENGTH
AT THE TRAILHEAD	**5.5 KM (ROUND-TRIP)**
🔍 HIGHLIGHTS	〰 ELEVATION GAIN
THE MOUNTAIN VILLAGE OF SALMO, THE WORLD'S OLDEST TELEPHONE BOOTH	**515 METERS**

OUT COLD
CREAM ALE

 STRAW YELLOW

 GRAINY

 DRY,
CORN,
GRAINY

BITTERNESS   SWEETNESS

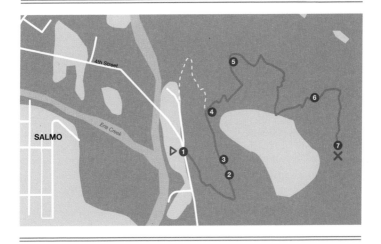

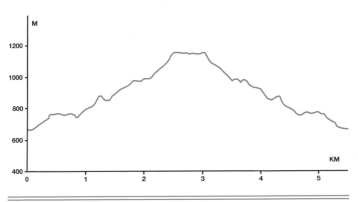

HIKE DESCRIPTION

Enjoy this workout of a hike that takes you to a succession of lofty views above a quaint village. On your return, sip a creamy ale brewed with the pristine, untreated water Salmo is known for.

The village of Salmo is nestled in the Selkirk mountains. If you're driving there from Creston, you'll be arriving via the Kootenay Pass, one of the highest passes on a major highway in Canada. You'll then descend into the village of Salmo, known as the "Hub of the Kootenays" because it's a thirty-minute drive from the surrounding communities of Nelson, Castlegar, Trail, and Creston. The name Salmo is Latin for salmon and was given to the area to avoid confusion with other places named after the salmon that swarmed freely through British Columbia before dams were built on the Columbia River in the 1960s. Salmo was originally called Salmon Siding and was founded as a mining town near the Nelson and Fort Sheppard Railway during the gold rush of 1896. Fun fact: Salmo is home to the world's oldest telephone booth, a public pay phone built into a 500-year-old cedar tree trunk.

Salmo survives primarily on tourism, but a stop here reveals that there is much more to the area than first meets the eye. The nearby Salmo Ski Hill, with its modest 340-meter vertical drop, even offers night skiing on fully illuminated slopes in the winter months. Combined with a little après-ski at Erie Creek Brewing, this could be a great way to spend an evening!

Our route to the Delaurentiis bluffs begins just minutes from town where Erie Creek flows into the Salmo River. The hike was named for the road at the bottom of the trail which, in turn, was named after one of the original families that lived along it. It's a steep and arduous climb that will get your heart pumping, but the viewpoints along the way make the effort worthwhile. You can choose to stop at any of the lower viewpoints if the ascent to the top seems too much. At the 1.2 km point, there are some loose rocks and boulders, and you'll have to mind your step, but it's not too difficult to navigate. To take your mind off those aching muscles, remember that you have an Out Cold Ale waiting for you minutes from the trailhead!

You'll need to purchase your trail pass online from the Salmo Valley Trail Society and then show your email receipt at the Erie Creek Brewery to pick up your trail pass sticker(s)—so don't forget to first check out the brewery's limited opening hours!

TURN-BY-TURN DIRECTION

1. From the sign and map in the parking lot, head straight up into the woods.
2. At 0.5 km, go right on the Bluffs Loop (marked by a black diamond).
3. At 0.6 km, reach a viewpoint with a bench.
4. At the junction at 0.9 km, go right, staying on the Bluffs Loop.
5. At 1.4 km, reach another viewpoint.
6. At 2.0 km, reach another viewpoint. This is also a good place to turn around if you don't want to go all the way to the top.
7. At 2.7 km, arrive at the viewpoint at the top of the bluffs. Return the way you came.

FIND THE TRAILHEAD

From Salmo, turn onto 4th Street and drive through town, crossing the Salmo River. After the bridge, at the point where Airport Road begins, reach a junction. Delaurentiis Road forks off to the left; follow it for 100 meters. The signed trailhead is on the right.

ERIE CREEK BREWING COMPANY

The water flowing into Salmo from the Selkirks is so pure that it requires no filtration when the village's only brewery produces its beer. The town has three aquifers—natural underground reservoirs that deliver pristine water to wells and springs. The owner of Erie Creek Brewing, Colin Hango, worked as a crane operator for nearly two decades; in 2014, he made his first batch of beer with a home brew kit and fell in love with the process. With some of the best water in the Rockies, tourists streaming through the town, and the wholehearted support of his community, Hango opened the doors of his nano-brewing company in 2020. One of Erie Creek's signature brews, Out Cold Cream Ale is named after a 2001 Hollywood parody filmed in Salmo.

LAND MANAGER

Salmo Valley Trail Society
PO Box 1125
Salmo, BC
V0G 1Z0
contact@salmovalleytrailsociety.org
www.salmovalleytrailsociety.org

BREWERY

Erie Creek Brewing Company
117 4th Street
Salmo, BC
VOG 1Z0
(250) 357-2479
Distance from trailhead: 1.2 kilometers

CRESTON MARSH LOOP AND A WILDLIFE WANDER

BIRDS, BULLRUSHES, AND A LUSH WETLAND STROLL

CRESTON
BC

▷··· STARTING POINT	···✗ DESTINATION
KOOTENAY COLUMBIA DISCOVERY CENTRE	**WILDLIFE TREE WANDER**
🍺 BREWERY	🔛 HIKE TYPE
WILD NORTH BREWING COMPANY	**EASY**
🐾 DOG FRIENDLY	📅 SEASON
YES (LEASH REQUIRED)	**YEAR-ROUND**
$ FEES	🕐 DURATION
NONE	**1 HOUR 45 MIN.**
🗺 MAP REFERENCE	↦ LENGTH
AT THE TRAILHEAD	**7.6 KM (LOOP)**
🔍 HIGHLIGHTS	〰 ELEVATION GAIN
MARSHLAND BOARDWALK, THREE-STOREY WILDLIFE LOOKOUT TOWER	**23 METERS**

KOOTENAY RIVER
RASPBERRY SOUR

6.0 %
ALCOHOL
CONTENT

HAZY BRIGHT PINK

FRESH RASPBERRIES

JAMMY,
FRUITY,
TART

BITTERNESS   SWEETNESS

5   5
4   4
3   3
2   2
1   1

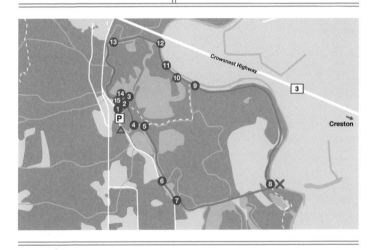

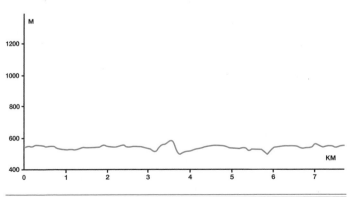

HIKE DESCRIPTION

Explore a unique Canadian river delta wetland that boasts a diversity of wildlife and spectacular scenery; then down a bright pink sour fruit bomb at Wild North's taproom.

The Creston Marsh Loop is located on a floodplain of the Kootenay River at the south end of Kootenay Lake in the Creston Valley Wildlife Management Area, a 7,000-hectare conservation area that lies just 10 kilometers north of the US border. The area is a designated Ramsar site—a wetland of international importance and an "Important Bird Area"—by BirdLife International. When you set foot onto the boardwalk at the trailhead, don't be surprised if you're greeted by a sudden rustling in the bushes and a burst of birdsong. In total, the area is home to 392 different wildlife species, including many fish, amphibians, birds, insects, and reptiles as well as deer, moose, elk, and bears. It supports over 100,000 waterbirds during migration periods, including greater white-fronted geese, tundra swans, American white pelicans, ospreys, and the "at risk" western grebes.

Not long into the hike, you can climb a three-storey wildlife lookout tower next to the marsh. You'll then continue through tall grasses and cattails as you make your way around ponds and along channels. Leaving the marsh area, you'll stroll amongst cottonwood trees on the Wildlife Tree Wander at the back end of the loop. The numerous small wooden structures along the route are nest boxes for tree swallows that are regularly monitored by wildlife specialists. And the big wooden box at the 5.5-kilometer point is what they call a "bat condo"! As the loop comes to an end, you'll enter a corridor of shrubs and trees on a stretch called Beaver Boulevard. You'll have marsh to both sides, so watch your step and stay on the path; it gets a little muddy. You may even spot some turtles! This area offers a variety of trails, allowing you to choose shorter or longer hikes, but the Marsh Loop gives you a lot of variety in a just a couple of hours. Enjoy!

TURN-BY-TURN DIRECTIONS

1. From the parking lot, walk a short distance to your left to step onto the boardwalk and into the marsh.
2. At 0.2 km, go right and cross the bridge.
3. At the intersection at 0.3 km, take the path to your right.
4. At 0.6 km, go right. The lookout tower will be on your left.
5. At 0.8 km, there's a map at the fork. Go right onto the path called Songbird Stroll.
6. At 1.4 km, turn left onto West Creston Road and follow it for 300 meters.
7. At 1.7 km, turn left onto the Wood Duck Walk, a double-track dirt path.
8. At 2.9 km, turn left onto the Wildlife Tree Wander.
9. At 5.0 km, continue straight ahead. The path naturally progresses onto the Marsh Trail.
10. At 5.3 km, take a short detour to a bird/duck watching area on the left; then retrace your steps back to the Marsh Trail.
11. At 5.6 km, pass a "bat condo" to your right.
12. At 5.8 km, turn left.
13. At 6.4 km, go left on the boardwalk and join Beaver Boulevard. There is a map on the left.
14. At 7.4 km, go right on the boardwalk and, almost immediately, right again over the bridge.
15. At 7.5 km, go left onto the gravel path. Step onto the boardwalk that returns to the parking lot.

FIND THE TRAILHEAD

From Creston, head north on 10th Avenue N and turn left on Pine Street. Turn right at the first crossroad onto BC-3 W and follow it for 500 meters. Turn left onto Valleyview Drive and follow it for 1 kilometer; then turn right onto Creston-Rykerts Highway/BC-21 N and proceed for 1.6 kilometers. Take a slight left onto BC-3 W (following signs for Salmo/Castlegar) and continue for about 7 kilometers; then turn left onto Creston Road. After 1 kilometer, reach the Kootenay Columbia Discovery Centre at the Creston Valley Wildlife Management Area.

WILD NORTH BREWING COMPANY

Husband-and-wife team Lisa and Craig Wood started Wild North Brewing with four high school friends from Creston. The town is home to international heavyweights—Labatt Brewing Company and the Columbia Brewery—but the founders recognized a need for a local small-batch craft brewery in the community. In 2021, in the middle of a global pandemic, they made the decision to provide a (safe) gathering place to sip delicious beer and share stories when their community needed it most. The team transformed an old bus stop into a brewery and taproom and hasn't looked back since. Settle in with a tart raspberry sour and pull a boardgame off the shelf for a perfect post-hike experience in the wild North.

As is true of many taprooms in the Rockies, dogs are allowed inside. Snacks are sold, but if you want to bring your own food or purchase from the food truck parked outside, be their guest!

LAND MANAGER

Creston Valley Wildlife Management Area
1874 Wildlife Road
Creston, BC
V0B 1G0
(250) 402-6900
www.crestonwildlife.ca

BREWERY

Wild North Brewing Company
125 16 Avenue N
Creston, BC
V0B 1G5
www.wildnorthbrewery.ca
Distance from trailhead: 13.2 kilometers

THE BEE LINE

A QUICK CLIMB TO 360-DEGREE VIEWS OF THE ROCKIES AND THE PURCELLS

STARTING POINT	DESTINATION
HIGHWAY 3/93/95	VIEWPOINT ON TOP OF UNNAMED HILL
BREWERY	HIKE TYPE
FISHER PEAK BREWING COMPANY	MODERATE
DOG FRIENDLY	SEASON
YES	YEAR-ROUND
FEES	DURATION
NONE	1.5 HOURS
MAP REFERENCE	LENGTH
CRANBROOK TOURISM	4.8 KM (LOLLIPOP LOOP)
HIGHLIGHTS	ELEVATION GAIN
VIEWS OF FISHER PEAK, A GRASSY PLATEAU	295 METERS

HELL ROARING SCOTTISH ALE

6.8 % ALCOHOL CONTENT

 MAHOGANY

 MALTY

 CREAMY CARAMEL, CHOCOLATE, COFFEE

BITTERNESS

SWEETNESS

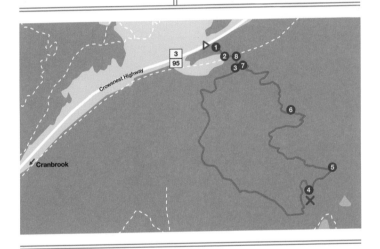

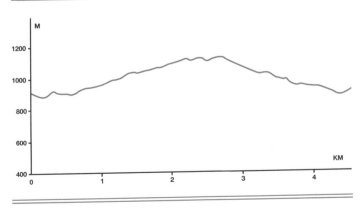

HIKE DESCRIPTION

Take a fun little trail to the top of an unnamed hill—because you know the view will be awesome! After you've worked up a sweat, sip the foam from a Hell Roaring Scottish ale for a taste of a best-in-class Canadian brew.

A local trail builder's motivation for building the Bee Line Trail was to create access to the best view of Fisher Peak (Mount Fisher), which, at an elevation of 2,842 meters, is the highest summit in the Southern Rocky Mountains. This prominent peak can be seen from the Crowsnest Highway and from Cranbrook, but it's worth your while hiking the 300 meters up to the unnamed buttes atop the Bee Line for the best vantage point, and for some great photos of the surrounding mountains, including the Steeples in the Hughes Range of the Canadian Rockies. The Bee Line is a short but fairly steep trail; its wildflower-filled meadows offer a reprieve as you climb above the tree line to an exposed grassy and rocky plateau. Be careful to not disturb any of the cairns that mark the trail.

Fisher Peak was named in 1920 after a British admiral, John Arbuthnot Fisher, who became known for reforming and modernizing the Royal Navy prior to World War I. Just before you start the up the Bee Line, you'll be walking the Chief Isadore Trail, named after the man who brokered peace between the Ktunaxa Nation and settlers in 1887. Once you've worked up a good thirst, make a beeline for the Fisher Peak Brewing Company!

TURN-BY-TURN DIRECTIONS

1. From the parking spot just off the highway, walk through the wooden gate leading into the woods and down a short hillside to another wooden gate and the gravel Chief Isadore Trail. Turn left onto the trail.

2. At 0.2 km, meet a narrow trail that crosses a creek and heads into the woods; it is marked by orange diamond blazes on trees. Take this trail.

3. At 0.3 km, you'll come to a log with a wooden sign reading "The Beeline." Go in the direction indicated by the sign.

4. At 2.3 km, reach a lookout with views of Fisher Peak and the Steeples.

5. At 2.5 km, reach a viewpoint of the bunchgrass-covered prairies below. From here, take a hard left on a trail marked by an orange blaze. After a short uphill climb, start your descent.

6. At 3.8 km, cross a double-track path. Go straight, following the orange blazes on the trees.

7. At 4.4 km, arrive back at the point where the loop began. Go right for about 100 meters and then turn left on the Chief Isadore Trail.

8. At 4.5 km, go through the gate on your right and up the hill to the parking spot.

FIND THE TRAILHEAD

To reach the parking area for the Bee Line Trail from Cranbrook, head north on BC-95/BC-3 toward Fort Steele for 7.1 km. You'll find the trail-head on the right side of the highway when you come to a rest stop. There's no signage and you can't see the trail from the road, so look for a pullout area with a wildlife-proof garbage bin that has space for 5–6 cars.

FISHER PEAK BREWING COMPANY

Before its transformation into a brewpub in 2013, the building housing the Fisher Peak Brewing Company was home to Heidi's Restaurant, an old-time schnitzelhaus run by Heidi Romich and her partner Marlies Romich. Now, the hybrid establishment houses both the Heid Out Restaurant (the restaurant's new name) and the Fisher Creek Brewing

Company, which is the Kootenay's only brewhouse. If you've worked up a hunger during your hike, you'll be pleased to know that when the brewery was established, the restaurant was also modernized and now showcases the talents of four Red Seal Chefs. Brewmasters Mark Simpson and Jordon Aasland are on site creating local craft beers that they say they would be proud to shout about from the mountain tops. It's quite possible that they had the Bee Line Trail in mind when they came up with that! Its Hell Roaring Scottish Ale is named after the nearby creek and follows the Heid-Out's protocol of using local names and events for its products. This Scotch Ale also won a gold medal in its category at the 2018 Canadian Brewing Awards.

LAND MANAGER

Cranbrook Community Forest
101 Kootenay Highway
East Kootenay C, BC
(877) 952-7277
www.cranbrookcommunityforest.com

BREWERY

Fisher Peak Brewing Company
821 Baker Street
Cranbrook, BC
V1C 1A2
(250) 426-7922
www.theheidout.ca/beer
Distance from trailhead: 6.2 kilometers

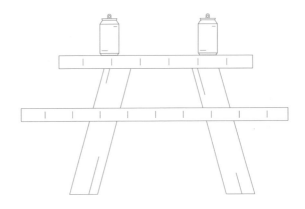

ROMANTIC RIDGE

BEAUTIFUL RIDGE WALK IN A NATURE PARK

KIMBERLEY
BC

▷⋯ STARTING POINT	⋯✗ DESTINATION
KIMBERLEY NATURE PARK, SWAN AVENUE TRAILHEAD	**ROMANTIC RIDGE**
🍺 BREWERY	HIKE TYPE
OVER TIME BEER WORKS	**MODERATE**
🐾 DOG FRIENDLY	📅 SEASON
YES	**YEAR-ROUND**
$ FEES	⏲ DURATION
NONE	**2 HOURS**
🗺 MAP REFERENCE	↦ LENGTH
AT TRAILHEAD	**6.3 KM (LOOP)**
🔍 HIGHLIGHTS	⌁ ELEVATION GAIN
CANADA'S HIGHEST CITY, A GERMAN YODELLING TIMEPIECE	**144 METERS**

 5.1 % ALCOHOL CONTENT

SPLIT WIT
BELGIUM WHITE

 STRAW WITH TOUCH OF
GRASSY-GREEN

 LIGHT MALT,
CLOVE,
SPICE

 ORANGE PEEL,
CLOVE,
CORIANDER

BITTERNESS   SWEETNESS

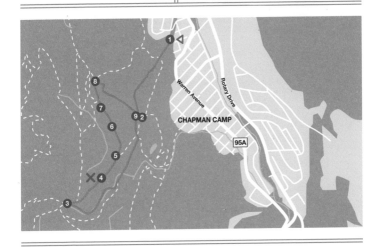

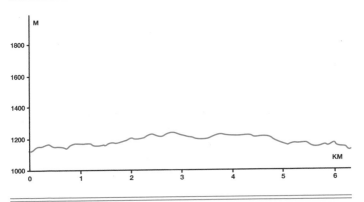

HIKE DESCRIPTION

Enjoy a moderate ridge climb with panoramic views in British Columbia's largest municipal park, followed by a spicy witbier that'll hit the spot as the weather changes and the leaves turn to gold.

The small city of Kimberley sits at the foothills of the Purcell Mountain Range in British Columbia. At 1,116 meters, it's Canada's highest city. In the Plazl (German for "piazza"), Kimberley's pedestrian zone, you might forget what country you're in as you gaze up at the world's largest freestanding cuckoo clock. If you happen to have a loonie (a Canadian one-dollar coin) in your pocket, pop it into the 6.7-meter-tall timepiece and watch a yodelling "Happy Hans" emerge to greet you. The German roots don't run deep in this part of the Rockies, however. In the 1970s, as local mines became depleted,

townsfolk in Kimberley faced the prospect of becoming a mining "ghost town" and decided to revamp the town's image to attract visitors. Today, the city depends more on its reputation as a recreational playground than on such gimmicks, however, and the province's largest municipal park, the Kimberley Nature Park, is a popular destination.

Despite its location in the middle of Kimberley, you'll feel like you're stepping deep into the wilderness when you walk the trails of this 840-hectare reserve. Don't be surprised if you spot mule and whitetail deer, moose, and elk. You may even see coyotes, cougars, wolves, and bears. The hike to Romantic Ridge is a heavily wooded ridgeline trail through a fir and larch forest, but it's not without its share of spectacular views. Because there are several branching trails in the park, having a map on hand is a good idea. This is one of the rare hikes on which you're not required to have dogs on a leash—but you are expected to clean up after them and ensure they don't harass wildlife.

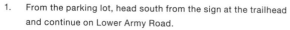

TURN-BY-TURN DIRECTIONS

1. From the parking lot, head south from the sign at the trailhead and continue on Lower Army Road.
2. At 1.2 km, reach Three Corners junction and go right on Lower Army Road.
3. At 2.6 km, go right on the narrow trail at the Romantic Ridge sign. (Continuing straight would take you to Upper Army Road.)
4. At 3.0 km, reach a fine viewpoint on the shoulder of Romantic Ridge.
5. At 3.2 km, look for the Romantic Ridge sign on your left. The Fall Line trail heads off to the right but continue downhill on the Romantic Ridge trail.
6. At 3.6 km, come into view of Kimberley through the trees on your right.
7. At 3.9 km, a sign for the Cabin Trail points to the left. Don't continue straight up the hill at this junction; instead, turn right onto the Patterson Ridge Trail.
8. At 4.2 km, turn right at the sign for Patterson Ridge. (Don't go straight on the Resident's Choice Trail.)
9. At 5.1 km, arrive back at Three Corners junction, which is the end of the loop. This time turn left to return to the trailhead.

FIND THE TRAILHEAD

Despite being at 180 Burdett Street, Kimberley, the trailhead is called the Swan Avenue Trailhead. To get there from the Kimberley Platzl, head southeast toward Wallinger Avenue. Turn right on Wallinger Avenue and follow it for 900 meters; then turn right on Burdett Street. The parking lot will be on the left after 230 meters, and the trailhead is at the far end of the parking lot.

OVER TIME BEER WORKS

Kenny Dodd, the owner of Over Time, is a Kimberley local who believes that no self-respecting mountain town with excellent water should exist without a craft brewery. There was something missing in this neck of the woods until 2016 when the doors of his brew works opened. Just steps from the Platzl, Over Time offers sales at the brewery, as well as off-sales in growlers and bulldogs. Post-hike, if you're game, you can play bocce in the brewery's own pit. And if you're there during the winter months, you can appreciate the mountain view from Over Time's heated outdoor patio! If you're wondering what to order, I suggest keeping your wits about you with the Split Wit, which is one of the brewery's tried-and-true standards, along with the golden and brown ales, and classic IPA. The brewers don't mess with a good thing, but they still play around with a few seasonal brews to keep the creative juices flowing.

LAND MANAGER

Kimberley Nature Park
St. Mary's Lake Road
Kimberley, BC
trails@kimberleynaturepark.ca
www.kimberleynaturepark.ca

BREWERY

Over Time Beer Works
136A Wallinger Avenue
Kimberley, BC
V1A 1Y8
(250) 427-2426
www.overtimebeer.ca
Distance from trailhead: 1 kilometer

GORBY TRAIL AND SHERWOODY LOOP

FOREST EXPLORATION IN MOUNT FERNIE PROVINCIAL PARK

MOUNT FERNIE
PROVINCIAL PARK, BC

▷··· STARTING POINT	···✕ DESTINATION
GORBY BRIDGE PARKING LOT	**"STEEP AND DEEP" SKI SLOPE**
🍺 BREWERY	🀄 HIKE TYPE
FERNIE BREWING COMPANY	**MODERATE** 🚶
🐾 DOG FRIENDLY	📅 SEASON
YES (LEASH REQUIRED)	**JUNE 1–SEPTEMBER 30**
$ FEES	🕐 DURATION
NONE (UNLESS CAMPING)	**2 HOURS 20 MIN.**
⛰ MAP REFERENCE	↦ LENGTH
AT TRAILHEAD	**7.7 KM (LOOP)**
🔍 HIGHLIGHTS	〰 ELEVATION GAIN
OLD-GROWTH CEDARS, GORBY BRIDGE	**275 METERS**

5.0 %
ALCOHOL
CONTENT

WHAT THE HUCK HUCKLEBERRY WHEAT ALE

 PINK GOLD

 LIGHT TART FRUIT,
MALT,
EARTHY

 BLUEBERRY,
MILD WHEAT,
SLIGHTLY TANGY

BITTERNESS

SWEETNESS

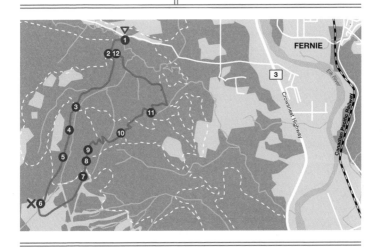

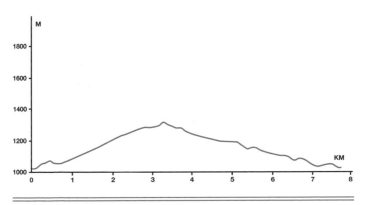

HIKE DESCRIPTION

Enjoy an alluring roam through forests and over ski runs; then cap your day with a taste of the wild at Fernie Brewing Company.

The trail name Gorby is a variant of Gorbies, an acronym coined in Banff before the Second World War to refer to "Great Outdoor Recreational Bastards in Every Sense." The ski patrol at Fernie started using the acronym (in the singular, as it were) to refer to the many people who needed to be rescued after skiing too far down into an area called Cedar Bowl. Consider yourself in on the joke now but rest assured that you won't be bothering the ski patrol or anyone else (except perhaps some wildlife) as you make your way along this jewel of a trail in Mount Fernie Provincial Park.

Don't be surprised when you encounter a painted tin goat impaled on a red stick early in the hike where the Gorby Trail diverges from the Old Goat Trail. Here, you can drop in a donation (or scan a QR code to do

so online) to support trail upkeep in Fernie. At the next trail to your left, step off Gorby for a few minutes to appreciate the magnificence of some stunning old and very large cedars. The old growth here isn't as prevalent as on the Old Growth Trail up the road but is still an exceptional part of the broad mix of flora this hike offers. (There are about 11.1 million hectares of old-growth forest in British Columbia. Coastal forests are generally considered old growth if they contain trees that are more than 250 years old; for interior forests, it's 140 years.)

The loop turns back just as you're entering the Fernie Alpine Resort ski area, and you'll see the "Steep and Deep" ski run just above you. It's a beautiful, wide-open space with lush meadows and wildflowers and a view down the valley. The view may be enough to entice you to return in the winter months to enjoy Fernie's exceptional alpine ski terrain. Look out for mountain bikers enjoying the fast, undulating descent through the trees as you finish up the loop.

TURN-BY-TURN DIRECTIONS

1. From the parking lot, cross Gorby bridge over Lizard Creek and immediately enter the forest.
2. At 0.3 km, stay right and begin the loop on the Gorby Trail.
3. At 1.3 km, at the junction with the Goat Trail (by the metal goat on a stick), continue straight on the Gorby Trail.
4. At 2.0 km, pass old-growth cedars off the trail to the left.
5. At 2.3 km, cross a ski area access road (Red Tree Road). Continue straight ahead on the Gorby Trail.
6. At 2.7 km, the trail begins to loop back at the "Steep and Deep" ski run. Enjoy the nice view down the valley.
7. At 3.5 km, there are many branching paths. Two ski trail signs on posts to the left point in different directions. One sign is green and reads "Ski View Trail," while the other is red and reads "Boomerang Chair." The path continues beneath these signs.
8. At 3.7 km, hit a road with a sign reading "Haul back T-bar." Cross the road and continue on the Gorby Trail.
9. At 3.8 km, turn left onto the Megahurtz Trail (there is a green sign on a tree here).
10. At 4.8 km, go left on the Happy Gilmar Trail.
11. At 5.8 km, go left at the intersection onto the Sherwood Trail.
12. At 7.4 km, turn right onto Gorby bridge and return to the trailhead and parking lot.

FIND THE TRAILHEAD

From Fernie, head southwest on BC-3 for 2.4 km and then turn right onto Mount Fernie Park Road. After 850 meters, reach the parking area on your right.

FERNIE BREWING COMPANY

The original Fernie-Fort Steele Brewing Company was founded way back 1898 in Fort Steele, which is now a heritage site 95 kilometers west of Fernie. Fort Steele, the first North-West Mounted Police fort in British Columbia, was established in 1864 during the Kootenay Gold Rush. The brewing company moved to Fernie in 1900; after a few name changes, buyouts, and consolidations, it closed in 1959. Beer wasn't brewed in Fernie again until 2003, when the Park family, long-time Fernie residents, started a brewery in their barn. In 2007, they realized their dream and opened for business at their current location, finally bringing craft brewing back to Fernie. They now distribute their beers throughout BC, Alberta, and Saskatchewan, and into Manitoba. Their vibrant "What the Huck" huckleberry wheat ale is made with real Rocky Mountain huckleberries and won third place in the fruit-beer category at the 2013 BC Beer Awards.

LAND MANAGER

EK Parks Ltd.
P.P. Box 118
6188 Wasa Lake Park Drive
Wasa, BC
V0B 2K0
(250) 422-3003
camping@ekparks.ca
www.ekparks.com

BREWERY

Fernie Brewing Company
26 Manitou Road
Fernie, BC
V0B 1M5
(250) 423-7797
www.ferniebrewing.com
Distance from trailhead: 8.0 kilometers

TURTLE MOUNTAIN

VIEW THE INFAMOUS FRANK SLIDE FROM TURTLE MOUNTAIN

BLAIRMORE
AB

▷⋯ STARTING POINT	⋯✗ DESTINATION
15TH AVENUE, BLAIRMORE	**NORTH PEAK, TURTLE MOUNTAIN**
⊓ BREWERY	HIKE TYPE
THE PASS BEER COMPANY	**STRENUOUS**
🐾 DOG FRIENDLY	SEASON
YES (LEASH REQUIRED)	**JUNE–OCTOBER**
$ FEES	🕐 DURATION
NONE	**2 HOURS 30 MIN.**
⌂ MAP REFERENCE	↦ LENGTH
WWW.CROWSNESTPASS.COM	**4.7 KM (ROUND-TRIP)**
🔍 HIGHLIGHTS	〜 ELEVATION GAIN
THE AFTERMATH OF THE FRANK LANDSLIDE, VIEWS OF THE CROWSNEST VALLEY	**411 METERS**

5.5 %
ALCOHOL CONTENT

COPPER
CONDUCTOR
VIENNA-STYLE
LAGER

COPPER

CARAMEL,
TOAST

CHOCOLATE,
SLIGHT ROAST,
BROWN SUGAR

BITTERNESS

SWEETNESS

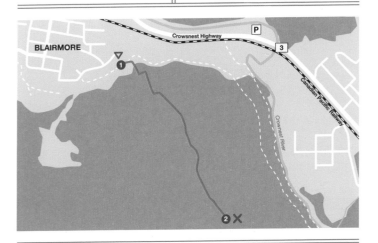

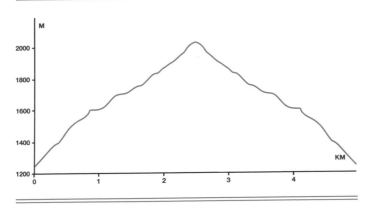

HIKE DESCRIPTION

Set off on a challenging climb to a summit with a view of Canada's deadliest rockslide. Then reward yourself with a lager and a pizza at the pass, your last chance for Alberta ale before crossing into BC.

In the early morning hours of April 29, 1903, Turtle Mountain collapsed without warning. The largest landslide in North American history and one of Canada's worst natural disasters, the event became known as the Frank slide, named after the town it buried. At least 76 people perished tragically in 100 seconds under the weight of 80 million tons of rock. The mountain itself, which had previously resembled the swell of a turtle's back, fractured into two distinct peaks with a chasm between them.

Our hike up Turtle Mountain ascends the northwest shoulder to the ridge from which the rock slid in 1903. The trail leads straight up to the 2,100-meter North Summit. It's a steep and challenging climb from the

start, and hiking poles are recommended. While not technically a scramble, the trail requires you to navigate some loose rocks along the way and involves walking relatively near sheer precipices.

Once you've hit the first peak, you have the option of continuing along the fractured summit ridge to the South (true) Summit, but this is for more advanced hikers who have scrambling experience. It will also add another two hours to the journey.

On the North Peak, the terrain levels out somewhat and the views are exceptional. From here, you can see the full extent of the Frank slide—the rubble of Turtle Mountain hasn't gone anywhere since it slid—and there's a lovely view of the Crowsnest Valley beyond. It can be quite windy up here, so be careful to not stand too close to the mountain's edge while taking in the view. Post-hike, after you've enjoyed your Copper Conductor and relaxed awhile, you may want to check out the Frank Slide Interpretive Center, just 5 kilometers east of Blairmore.

TURN-BY-TURN DIRECTIONS

1. The trailhead is marked by a yellow post and by painted yellow rocks. From here, the trail is straightforward all the way to the summit.

2. At 2.4 km, reach the viewpoint on the North Summit. Return the way you came.

FIND THE TRAILHEAD

In Blairmore, a small town just west of Frank on the Crowsnest Highway (Highway 3), turn left on 133 Street; follow it to its end and turn left onto 15 Street. When you reach 134 Street, turn right on a road that progresses back into 15 Street. Take the first dirt road on your right (a powerline right of way) and park anywhere along this road. From where the dirt road comes to an end, continue walking in the same direction, now on a dirt path leading toward the trees. The path narrows and veers upward and to the right before coming to a yellow post (the trailhead) on the edge of the trees.

THE PASS BEER COMPANY

The Pass Beer Company in Blairmore, in the municipality of Crowsnest Pass, is located 20 kilometers east of the provincial border. This is your last chance to enjoy Alberta craft beer before crossing over into British Columbia, or your first opportunity to imbibe in Alberta, if coming from the other direction! The owners of Pass, Danielle and Tony Radvak, opened the brewery in 2020; it was awarded a bronze medal in the New Brewery of the Year category at the 2021 Alberta Beer Awards. Danielle formerly ran a successful home-based business while Tony is a professional glazier. Of their decision to found their own brewery, Danielle explains, "Tony just really likes beer and talked about opening a brewery for years. As we have kids and a husky, we wanted to have a place that was welcoming, comfortable, and family- and pet-friendly." The two also share a love for Neapolitan-style wood-fired pizza, so Danielle headed to Los Angeles for a crash course in making just that. So, while you refresh with your lager or any of Pass's other enticing flagship beers, you'll be entertained by a chef tossing and twirling pizza dough just off the taproom. The brewery also serves poutine, wings, salads, and nachos. Ninety percent of its food is made from scratch, and the ingredients are locally sourced whenever possible.

LAND MANAGER

Crowsnest Pass
8502 19th Avenue
Coleman, AB
T0K 0E0
(403) 562-8833
www.crowsnestpass.com

BREWERY

The Pass Beer Company
10801 20th Avenue
Blairmore
Crowsnest Pass, AB
T0K 0E0
(403) 753-1100
www.passbeer.ca
Distance from trailhead: 3 kilometers

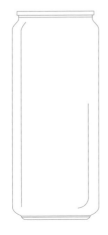

ACKNOWLEDGMENTS

I'd like to thank everyone who has supported me on my beer hiking journey: my sister Mystee and her husband Rick, without whose generosity I literally could not have completed this book; my dad, for sharing ideas over coffee—numerous times; the crew at Banff Tea Co. for accommodating my schedule and lending me wheels when I needed them; all the brewery owners and staff who gave me their time and attention; my editor Ashley Curtis for his attentiveness when words (and punctuation) failed; and the folks at Helvetiq for conceptualizing a series that set me on such a fun and interesting path through the beautiful Rockies. Finally, a thank you to my "trail markers," my daughters Sadie and Jemima, who, with their love and support, have led me over the most challenging mountains and through the darkest valleys. You are the reason.

BEER HIKING
PACIFIC NORTHWEST
THE TASTIEST WAY TO DISCOVER
WASHINGTON, OREGON, AND BRITISH COLUMBIA

NEW AND
UPDATED
EDITION

RACHEL WOOD
BRANDON FRALIC

45 MIN.

52 CRAFT BREWERIES
HANDPICKED HIKES

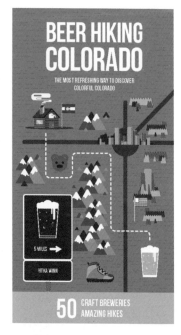

BEER HIKING
COLORADO
THE MOST REFRESHING WAY TO DISCOVER
COLORFUL COLORADO

5 MILES

YITKA WINN

50 CRAFT BREWERIES
AMAZING HIKES

RANDOS BIÈRE
AU QUÉBEC
LA FAÇON LA PLUS RAFRAÎCHISSANTE DE VOIR LE QUÉBEC

12 KM →

BIANCA POMERLEAU

BEER HIKING
NEW ENGLAND
THE TASTIEST WAY TO DISCOVER MAINE,
NEW HAMPSHIRE, VERMONT, MASSACHUSETTS,
CONNECTICUT AND RHODE ISLAND

CAREY KISH

← 20 MIN.

50 CRAFT BREWERIES
HANDPICKED HIKES